THIS BOOK WILL MAKE YOU A SCIENTIST

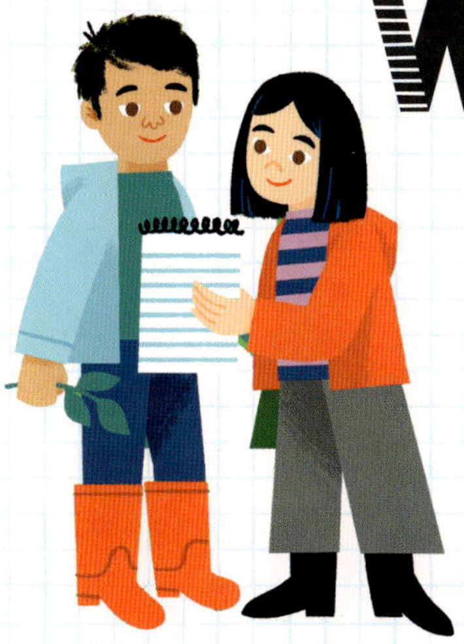

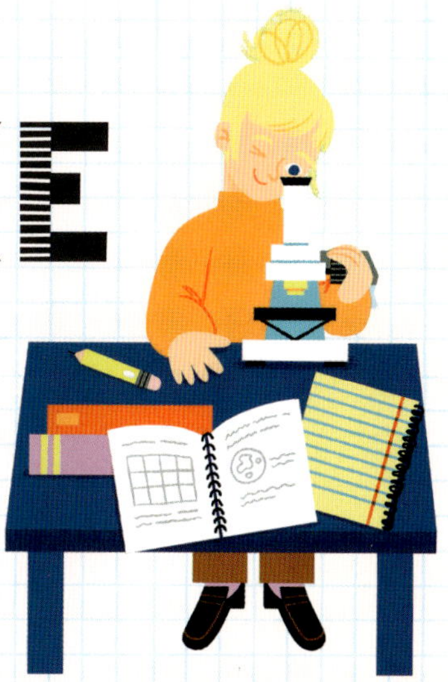

WRITTEN BY
Dr Sheila Kanani

ILLUSTRATED BY
Ellen Surrey

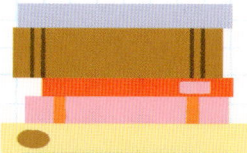

To the children of the world. You are all scientists! Engineer your own happiness and change the world with kindness.
S. K.

For all the future scientists, may this book inspire you.
E. S.

With thanks to the following people at the University of Cambridge for their contribution and advice:
the team at the Whipple Museum of the History of Science; Dr N. Baker-Campbell of the Department of Physics;
Dr Matthew Bothwell of the Institute of Astronomy; Dr Jinx St. Léger of the Department of Engineering;
Dr Douglas Palmer of the Sedgwick Museum of Earth Sciences.

First published 2026 by Nosy Crow Ltd
Wheat Wharf, 27a Shad Thames,
London, SE1 2XZ, UK

Nosy Crow Eireann Ltd
c/o Fieldfisher Ireland LLP
45 Mespil Road, Dublin 4,
D04 W2F1, Ireland

www.nosycrow.com

ISBN 978 1 80513 254 7

Nosy Crow and associated logos are trademarks
and/or registered trademarks of Nosy Crow Ltd.

Text © Sheila Kanani 2026
Illustrations © Ellen Surrey 2026

The right of Sheila Kanani to be identified as the author and Ellen Surrey
to be identified as the illustrator of this work has been asserted.

All rights reserved.

This book is sold subject to the condition that it shall not, by way of trade or otherwise,
be lent, hired out or otherwise circulated in any form of binding or cover other than that in
which it is published. No part of this publication may be reproduced, stored in a retrieval system,
or transmitted in any form or by any means (electronic, mechanical, photocopying, recording
or otherwise) without the prior written permission of Nosy Crow Ltd.

The publisher and copyright holders prohibit the use of
either text or illustrations to develop any generative machine learning
artificial intelligence (AI) models or related technologies.

A CIP catalogue record for this book is available from the British Library.

Printed in China following rigorous ethical sourcing standards.

1 3 5 7 9 8 6 4 2

CONTENTS

Introduction	4–11
Make perfume like **TAPPUTI-BELATEKALLIM**	12–13
Measure volumes like **ARCHIMEDES**	14–15
Make a rainbow like **KAMĀL AL-DĪN AL-FĀRISĪ**	16–17
Create a pendulum like **GALILEO GALILEI**	18–19
Find the centre of gravity like **ISAAC NEWTON**	20–21
Search for stars like **CAROLINE HERSCHEL**	22–23
Make invisible ink like **JAMES JAY**	24–25
Explore evolution like **CHARLES DARWIN**	26–27
Search for fossils like **MARY ANNING**	28–29
Make static electricity like **NIKOLA TESLA**	30–31
Test acids and alkalines like **S. P. L. SØRENSEN**	32–33
Collect plants like **YNÉS MEXÍA**	34–35
Measure the speed of light like **ALBERT EINSTEIN**	36–37
Grow mould like **ALEXANDER FLEMING**	38–39
Blend oil like **ALICE BALL**	40–41
Make crystals like **DOROTHY HODGKIN**	42–43
Extract DNA like **ROSALIND FRANKLIN**	44–45
Measure your heartbeat like **MARIE MAYNARD DALY**	46–47
Make a crater like **EUGENE MERLE SHOEMAKER**	48–49
Communicate with chimpanzees like **JANE GOODALL**	50–51
Watch a volcano erupt like **KATIA KRAFFT**	52–53
Design an aeroplane like **CHRISTINE DARDEN**	54–55
Study black holes like **STEPHEN HAWKING**	56–57
Train to be an astronaut like **MAE JEMISON**	58–59
Test a space-landing like **RITU KARIDHAL**	60–61
Glossary	62–63
About the Author and Illustrator	64

INTRODUCTION

THIS BOOK WILL MAKE YOU A SCIENTIST! YES, YOU!

As you turn the pages, you will meet scientists from the past and the present, from different cultures, locations and places in the world. Discover biologists, chemists, physicists, astronomers, astronauts and more, who have all invented, created or discovered incredible science!

But how did they think up their exciting experiments? When did they start to wonder about how the world works? And why did these people become so fascinated by dinosaurs, birds, volcanoes and black holes? Asking questions is the first step to becoming a scientist, and finding out some of the answers might even give you some ideas to create your own experiments!

You will discover what makes a good scientist and what different scientists do. You will learn about what inspired them to study their area of science – whether that is making crystals, hunting for fossils, investigating unusual places all over the world, or even taking trips into space! Whether these scientists studied nature, chemicals, light or electricity, you can be sure of one thing: all scientists are curious and love to discover new things!

Scientists are very good at working together in teams. This is called 'collaboration', and sometimes, without teamwork, the science just can't get done! So perhaps you might like to use this book, and the experiments in it, to work with your friends and family in a team.

There are many different types of science. Some of the people in this book were the first to do their experiments. Others took what previous scientists had learned and expanded their knowledge. Some will have worked together, and others worked alone.

You may have learned about some of these ideas before, but you will also discover brand-new theories and concepts. Some of these words might be new to you, but this book is here to teach you the terms and language that scientists use!

Most importantly of all, this book will let you learn about science through doing it! After meeting each of the scientists in the book, you will be able to conduct your own experiments to create electricity like Nikola Tesla, extract DNA like Rosalind Franklin, design an aeroplane like Christine Darden, and much, much more!

**Now it's your turn!
Be inspired by this book
and become a scientist . . .**

GETTING STARTED IN YOUR LABORATORY

From lying in the bath to soaring through space, the scientists in this book have worked anywhere and everywhere. In this book, you will meet Tapputi-Belatekallim who made herb perfumes in ancient Mesopotamia, Katia Krafft who studied volcanoes around the world and Jane Goodall who spent months in the jungle with chimpanzees!

Throughout history, many scientists have also worked from a special place called a laboratory, or lab. Inside this space, a scientist can carry out experiments on their own, or with others.

Scientists might do small experiments on the laboratory desk, or need giant computers to help them with their calculations. They might use different equipment, such as pipettes, electrical wires or magnets, or they might need nothing more than a pencil and some paper. Sometimes scientists will spend weeks on their work, and sometimes their experiments will take them a lifetime, hidden from the world until they feel that they've found the answers to all the questions they can think of! A lab can be anywhere – even in your bedroom or kitchen.

In a laboratory, scientists will usually keep their equipment, tools, books and other useful objects. They might also have personal items to keep them motivated, such as photos of the people who inspire them. What else do you think a scientist might keep in their laboratory?

WHAT WILL YOU NEED TO DO YOUR SCIENCE EXPERIMENTS?

In this book, you will read about all sorts of different things that you can use for your experiments, from toothpicks and toilet roll, to strawberries and seashells!

For many of the activities in the book, you will only need a few items, most of which can be found in the kitchen. However, you will also need some tools and materials like those on this page.

Some tools and materials you might need:

Scissors

A pen

Colouring pencils

Glass cups and jars

Card

Paper

Erase

Keeping clean
Science experiments can be messy sometimes! It's a good idea to have an apron or old T-shirt to cover your clean clothes, and some newspaper or a wipe-clean tablecloth to protect your home.

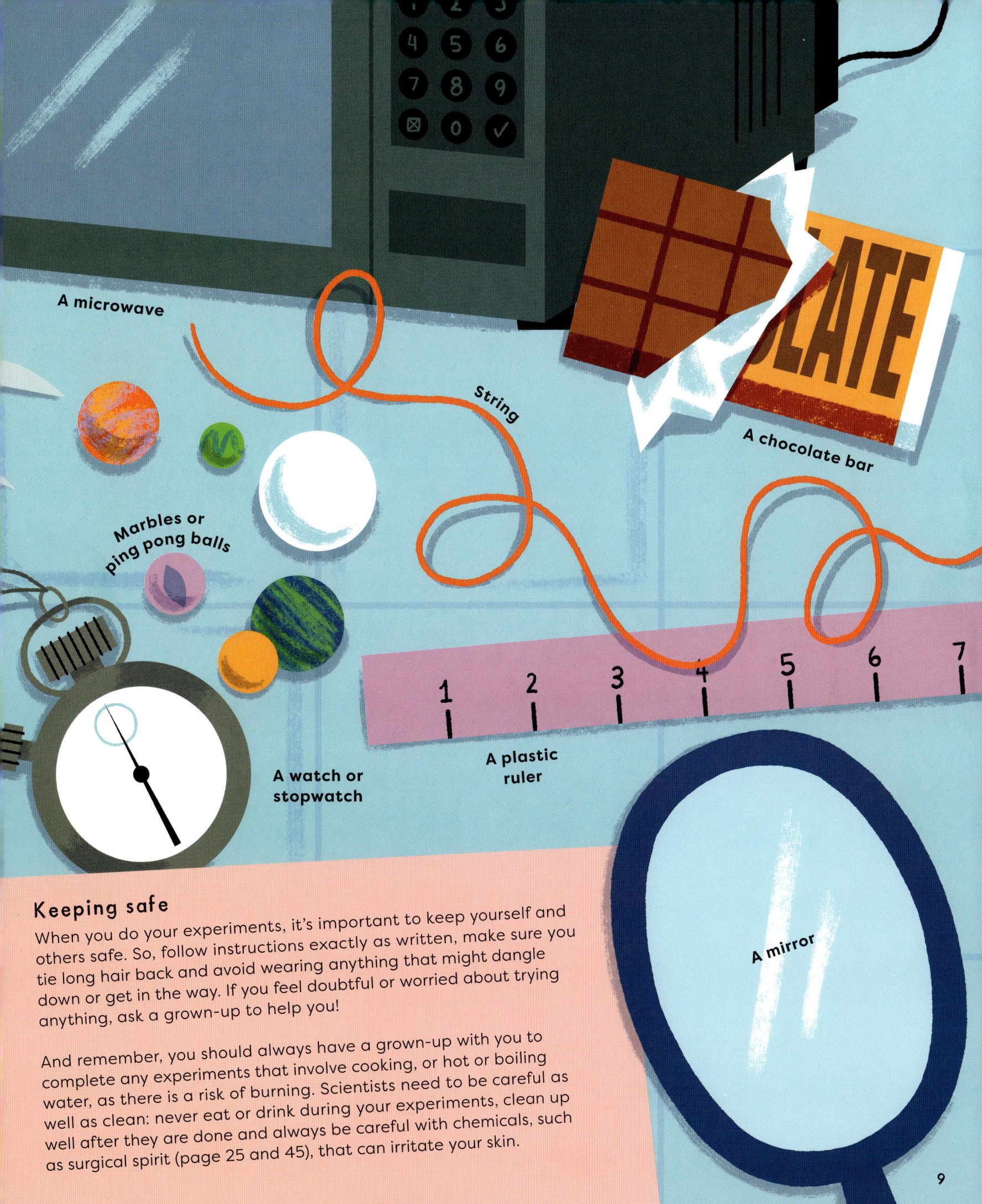

A microwave

A chocolate bar

String

Marbles or ping pong balls

A watch or stopwatch

A plastic ruler

A mirror

Keeping safe

When you do your experiments, it's important to keep yourself and others safe. So, follow instructions exactly as written, make sure you tie long hair back and avoid wearing anything that might dangle down or get in the way. If you feel doubtful or worried about trying anything, ask a grown-up to help you!

And remember, you should always have a grown-up with you to complete any experiments that involve cooking, or hot or boiling water, as there is a risk of burning. Scientists need to be careful as well as clean: never eat or drink during your experiments, clean up well after they are done and always be careful with chemicals, such as surgical spirit (page 25 and 45), that can irritate your skin.

TRY, TRY AND TRY AGAIN!

Many of the scientists in this book have had to try many times to get their experiments to work successfully, making mistakes and learning from them along the way. And sometimes, just sometimes, it is the *mistake* that ends up becoming the incredible scientific discovery. You will read about one scientist who forgot to tidy up his lab before going on holiday, only to come back and realise he had created a miracle drug!

Before you start the experiments in this book, you can practise some basic science skills. These are the building blocks for becoming a better scientist.

1. Exploration and observation

Take a walk through nature and explore your surroundings. What can you see? What can you hear? What can you smell? Use your senses to explore where you are. Everywhere is a laboratory, and this is a great way to start training your brain to think scientifically.

2. Measuring and pouring

Use different objects and ways of measuring and pouring. You could pour water from a bottle into a cup. You could weigh some food and compare it to other objects. How tall are you? How tall is a tree? Using numbers to measure is a good way to practise using scientific language!

3. Using tools

Hands-on experiments are great practice for scientific thinking. What tools might you need? Rulers, weighing scales, paperclips, pencils – these are all scientific tools!

Some scientists have had to try again and again to have their ideas and experiments taken seriously. You will read about scientists who were not believed at first because of their gender or skin colour, and you will read about scientists whose findings were so incredible or unusual that people couldn't believe they were correct.

So, if you'd like to become a scientist, you will need to have the patience, confidence and determination to believe in yourself and try, try and try again!

4 Asking questions

Spark your curiosity by asking lots of questions! Think about the 'why' and the 'how' when you look at something. There are so many questions out there to ask! Why is the sky blue? How deep is the sea? Why do we dream? How clever are animals?

5 Predictions and estimations

Can you find patterns in things (such as animal prints or leaves) and then use those patterns to work out what might come next? Could you look at something and estimate how big it is, or how much of it there is? How long do you think it might take water to boil? Can you make a guess, then have a go and find out? Practise these skills and think like a scientist!

6 Gathering and recording information, or 'data'

Information is often known as 'data'. How will you gather the data you've found out? Will you write it down? Or can you draw it? Can you group different things together by colour or type, or look for the odd one out?

7 Communicating

Sharing your science helps others learn too! And words aren't the only way to communicate – you could draw pictures and charts too. What about a short video explaining what you've discovered?

Make perfume like TAPPUTI-BELATEKALLIM

Tapputi-Belatekallim was the world's first recorded **CHEMIST**. She lived in Mesopotamia, in modern-day Iraq, and worked as a royal perfume-maker. We know about her because she is mentioned in an ancient piece of writing, known as a cuneiform tablet, which was written around 1200 BCE!

To make her perfumes, Tapputi would mix flowers, natural oils, herbs and tree sap with water and other liquids, before 'distilling' the mixture. Distilling is when you separate out different substances by boiling a mixture until it evaporates (turns into a gas) and then cooling it so that the water vapour turns back into a liquid. The equipment you need to do this is called a 'still', and Tapputi used, and possibly even built, the first ever documented still for this process.

NOW IT'S YOUR TURN!

What you will need:

- Fresh water
- Flower petals such as rose or honeysuckle
- Herbs such as lavender or rosemary
- Muslin or cheesecloth
- A rolling pin or mallet
- A small glass bowl
- A small bottle or jar
- A small colander
- A cooking pot with a domed lid

1 Place your flower petals and herbs on a piece of muslin or cheesecloth. Ask a grown-up to help you crush them with a rolling pin or mallet, then cover the petals up with the rest of the muslin or cheesecloth.

2 Add a small amount of water to the cooking pot (around five centimetres deep) and place a colander inside the pot so that the water level sits just below the bottom of the colander.

Tapputi's perfumes weren't just for smelling nice. Ancient people believed that these beautiful scents could travel up to the gods and make them happy. They also used perfumed ointments to heal injuries and illnesses.

Tapputi needed a deep understanding of chemistry to do her job. A lot of the equipment and ingredients for the perfumes were originally used in the kitchens, and by women. It is likely that most early chemists were women.

Tapputi was revolutionary in her methods, even creating a new technique to make her perfumes last longer and smell brighter than before. Today, chemical engineers use many of the same techniques that Tapputi used 3,000 years ago.

3 Place the muslin or cheesecloth parcel inside the colander and then put a small glass bowl on top of it.

4 Put the lid on top of the pot, upside down so that the domed lid is directly on top of the small glass bowl.

5 Ask your grown-up to help you heat the pot on a low heat. As the water heats up, it will evaporate and condense (turn back into liquid) when it touches the upside-down lid.

TIP: Place ice in the middle of the upside-down lid to speed up the condensation!

6 Your perfume will drip from the upside-down lid into the small glass bowl. When all the water in the pot has evaporated, turn the heat off and leave everything to cool.

7 Transfer your distilled perfume into a small bottle or jar and enjoy!

Measure volumes like ARCHIMEDES

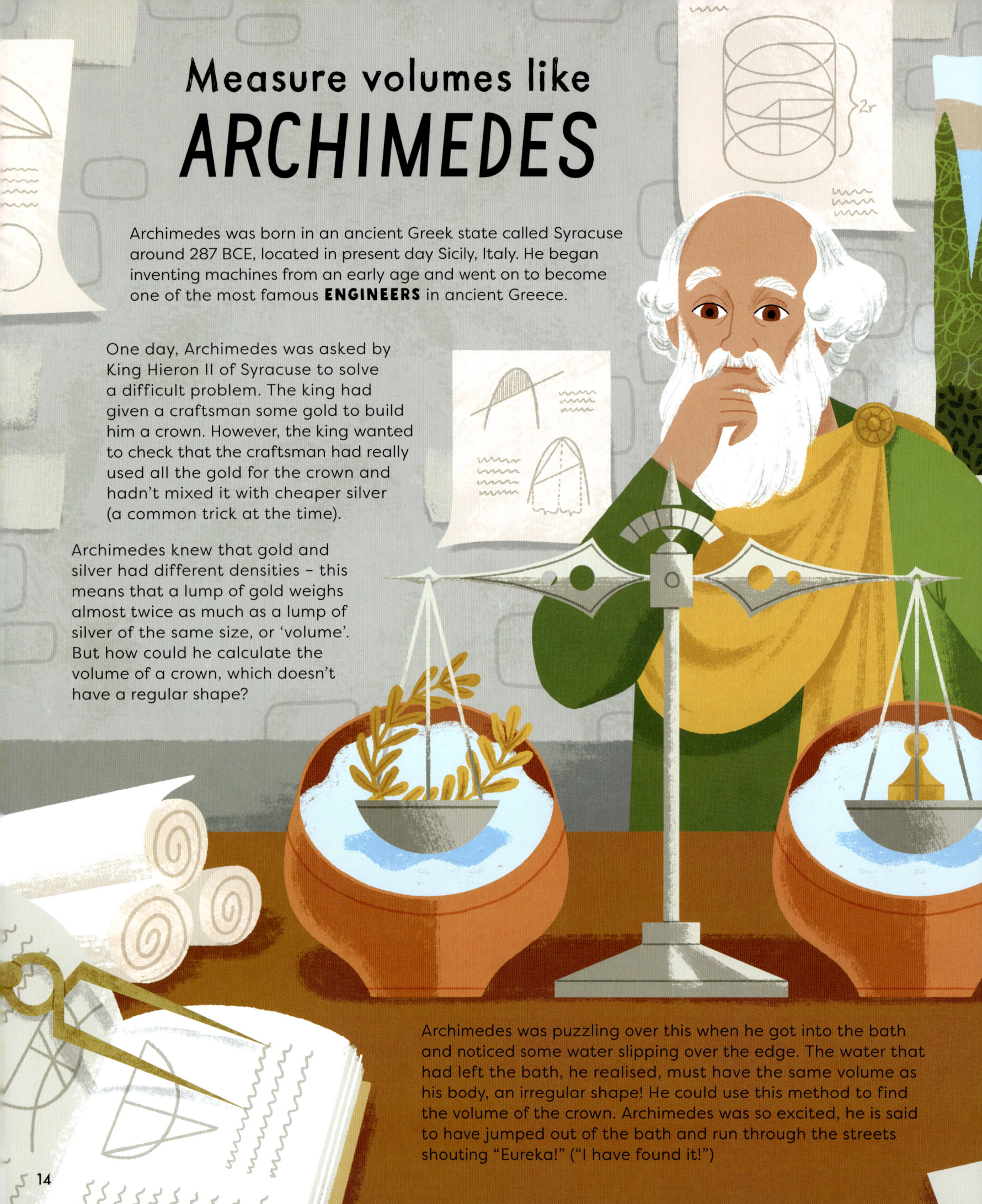

Archimedes was born in an ancient Greek state called Syracuse around 287 BCE, located in present day Sicily, Italy. He began inventing machines from an early age and went on to become one of the most famous **ENGINEERS** in ancient Greece.

One day, Archimedes was asked by King Hieron II of Syracuse to solve a difficult problem. The king had given a craftsman some gold to build him a crown. However, the king wanted to check that the craftsman had really used all the gold for the crown and hadn't mixed it with cheaper silver (a common trick at the time).

Archimedes knew that gold and silver had different densities – this means that a lump of gold weighs almost twice as much as a lump of silver of the same size, or 'volume'. But how could he calculate the volume of a crown, which doesn't have a regular shape?

Archimedes was puzzling over this when he got into the bath and noticed some water slipping over the edge. The water that had left the bath, he realised, must have the same volume as his body, an irregular shape! He could use this method to find the volume of the crown. Archimedes was so excited, he is said to have jumped out of the bath and run through the streets shouting "Eureka!" ("I have found it!")

Using his knowledge of levers and pulleys, Archimedes created weapons and defences to protect the people of Syracuse from the Romans. Sadly, though, he was killed aged 75. In some stories, Archimedes was drawing mathematical pictures in the sand when a Roman soldier snuck up on him. It is said that his last words were "Don't disturb my circles!"

NOW IT'S YOUR TURN!

What you will need:

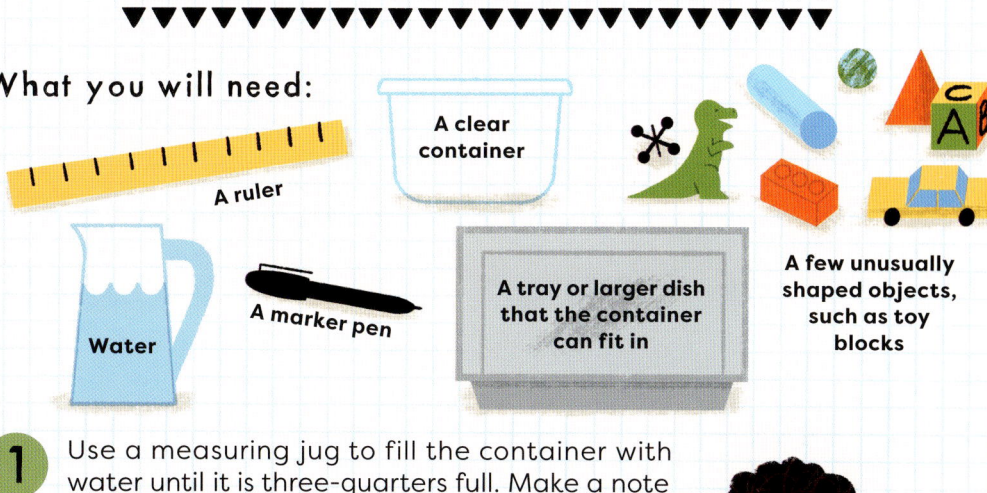

- A ruler
- A clear container
- Water
- A marker pen
- A tray or larger dish that the container can fit in
- A few unusually shaped objects, such as toy blocks

1 Use a measuring jug to fill the container with water until it is three-quarters full. Make a note of the volume (amount) of water in the container, such as 'one litre'. Place the container in the tray or larger dish to catch any spills.

2 Mark a line on the container with a marker pen to show the current level of the water. Measure the height from the base to your line with a ruler.

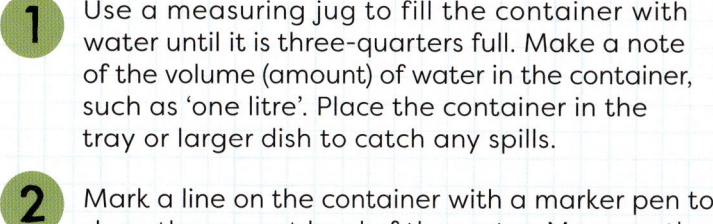

3 Submerge your object in the water.

4 The water level will have risen! With a ruler, measure the distance between the new water level and the marker line you made. This is the amount of water displacement.

5 Now that you know the water displacement, you can find out what the volume of the object is with this sum: multiply the displacement by the volume of water you put in the tub, and divide that by the height you first measured.

6 You have found the volume of the object that you submerged! Eureka!

Make a rainbow like KAMĀL AL-DĪN AL-FĀRISĪ

Kamāl al-Dīn al-Fārisī was a Persian **ASTRONOMER**, born around 1267, who used a special object called a camera obscura to study rainbows.

A camera obscura is a dark room, or box, with a small hole in one wall or side. Because the light comes in from the hole, an upside-down picture of what is outside is created on the opposite wall.

Al-Fārisī used a camera obscura to look very closely at how a rainbow is formed. Previous scientists thought that rainbows were made from sunlight reflected by clouds. Al-Fārisī thought differently – he believed that a ray of light from the Sun would bounce from raindrop to raindrop and become bent, creating the rainbow.

Al-Fārisī carried out an experiment to prove his theory. He filled a large spherical vase with water, and placed it in a camera obscura, to create rainbows.

But he wasn't able to work out exactly why this happened, nor explain why or how the bending of light could make the colours in the rainbow.

Before Al-Fārisī, people thought you could get different colours of light by mixing light and dark, whereas Al-Fārisī went on to prove that the colours were formed by mixing and bending the light on a dark background.

It is possible that camera obscuras date back to before 400 BCE, and they have helped us understand how light travels, as well as how our eyes work.

NOW IT'S YOUR TURN!

What you will need:

- A small mirror
- A torch
- Water
- A glass
- A piece of white paper

1 Fill a glass with water and put the mirror in the water.

2 Take the glass and the paper to a place where's there's not much light. Shine the torch toward the centre of the mirror.

3 Hold the glass above the paper or place it on the paper.

4 Watch the torch light pass through the glass, bending the light and forming rainbows on the paper.

5 Experiment with different distances, heights and angles to see if you can make better rainbows.

Create a pendulum like GALILEO GALILEI

Galileo Galilei was born in 1564 in Pisa, Italy. When Galileo was 19, he was at the cathedral in Pisa watching a chandelier swinging. He timed it using his pulse and realised that, as the chandelier swung, it always kept the same time. Back then, clocks were not very reliable. As Galileo watched the chandelier, he realised how he could make a clock keep time much better: by adding a pendulum!

Galileo was working as a **MATHS** professor when he heard about the invention of the telescope. He decided to make his own, bigger version, with better magnifying power. It allowed him to see objects in space in ways that no one had ever been able to! In 1610, Galileo saw Jupiter and its four largest moons. He saw craters on the Moon, and the stars of the Milky Way.

At this time, most people believed that all the planets moved around the Earth. Galileo disagreed with this. He had seen the moons moving around Jupiter through his telescope, and he loudly supported the views of an astronomer called Copernicus, who had declared that the planets, including Earth, move around the Sun.

The Roman Catholic Church, who held a lot of power and could act like the police, didn't agree with these ideas at all. They gave Galileo a strong warning, but he didn't change his mind, and he ended up being arrested for his views.

As he got older, Galileo became blind, but he continued his work until he died in 1642. It wasn't until 350 years after his death that he was pardoned by the church for supporting the fact that everything orbited around the Sun.

NOW IT'S YOUR TURN!

What you will need:
* A paper cup
* Scissors
* String
* Sticky tape
* A broom handle or long stick
* 2 kitchen chairs
* Salt or sand (enough to nearly fill your cup)
* A clock or watch

1 Ask a grown-up to poke a hole on either side of the rim of the cup.

2 Cut a long piece of string. Thread the ends of the string through the holes then tie the ends together to make a large loop, as if it is a handle for the cup.

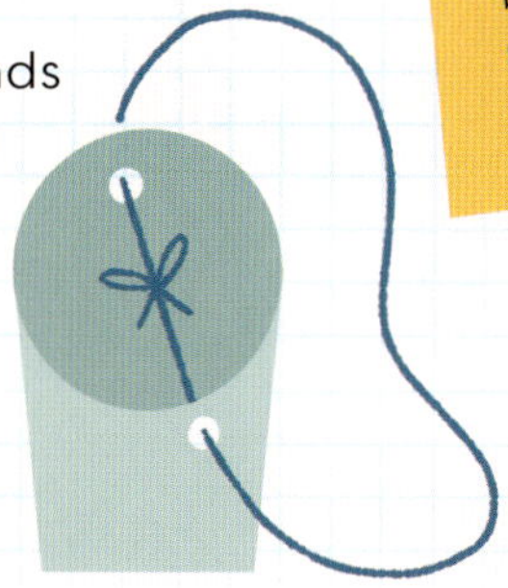

3 Slide the stringed cup onto the stick or broom handle and balance the stick or broom handle across two chairs.

4 Fill the cup with salt or sand.

TIP: You could fill the cup with paint and poke a hole in the bottom of the cup, and as the pendulum swings, it would create pendulum paint art beneath! Just make sure you lay paper all over the floor!

5 Push the cup gently so it swings from side to side, and try to measure if the swing of the pendulum keeps to time!

Find the centre of gravity like ISAAC NEWTON

Isaac Newton was born in the UK on Christmas Day in 1643. He grew up on a farm, but as a child he was far more interested in building sundials and watermills than farming, so he went to study at the University of Cambridge.

Newton loved learning about **PHYSICS**, maths, optics (the behaviour of light) and astronomy (the study of stars, planets and other objects in the universe). When the Great Plague hit in 1665, he had to return home to his family farm, but he didn't give up on his studies.

According to one story, while Newton was in his garden one day, he saw an apple fall from a tree. It sparked a question in his mind: what was it that made the apple fall to the ground, rather than in different directions? Newton realised the force that had brought the apple crashing down (gravity) is the same force that keeps the planets in orbit!

NOW IT'S YOUR TURN!

What you will need:
* 2 metal forks
* Toothpicks
* A glass

1. Wedge the two forks together by their tines (prongs).

2. Balance the forks on your finger to find the mid-point.

3. Insert the cocktail stick in between the tines at the mid-point.

4. Place the other end of the cocktail stick on the rim of the glass. Slide the cocktail stick backwards and forwards along the rim until you find the balance point.

5. You have found the centre of gravity of the two forks! It is directly below the rim of the glass where the toothpick is balanced. This is known as the 'pivot point'.

TIP: Though you can't see the centre of gravity of the system, you know you've found it because the whole system is balanced.

Using his maths skills, Newton developed something called 'calculus', which is a way of calculating answers from numbers that are continually changing. Newton was also really interested in colour and light. He was able to show that when you split up white light, it contains all the colours in the rainbow.

Newton died in 1727, aged 84, and he was buried at Westminster Abbey in London. He was the first scientist to be given such an honour!

Search for stars like CAROLINE HERSCHEL

Caroline Herschel was born in 1750 in Hanover, Germany. When she was little, she became very poorly with an illness called typhus. This meant that Herschel didn't grow very tall. Her mother didn't believe that girls should go to school, so instead, Herschel spent her childhood cleaning, cooking and looking after the family house.

When Herschel grew older, her brother William moved to the UK to be a musician, and he asked her to come with him to sing in his choir. She jumped at the chance, and they moved to Bath, where Herschel quickly became an excellent musician. When William began studying planets and stars, however, Herschel turned down a career in music to work alongside him.

NOW IT'S YOUR TURN!

What you will need:
- A notebook
- A pen
- Warm clothes
- A torch to find your way there and back

1. Wait for an evening when the night sky is clear, and the weather is good. With an adult, go to an open space away from any lights.

2. Make yourself comfortable and safe, and allow your eyes to adapt to the darkness. You might need to wear warm clothes.

A comet is a chunk of ice and dust that travels around the Sun.

Herschel helped William build telescopes to find new and exciting things in the sky, such as the planet Uranus! She would work all day then spend all night searching the sky for stars and creating a list that astronomers still use today. One night, Herschel saw something different – it wasn't a star, but a comet! She went on to spot eight comets in total.

With Herschel's help, William built larger and larger telescopes, eventually making the largest telescope in the world at that time at 12 metres long.

Herschel was paid by King George III for her role as assistant to William. This made her the first woman in England with an official government position, and the first woman to be paid for her work in **ASTRONOMY**.

Herschel moved back to Germany when she was older and, in 1828, the Royal Astronomical Society presented her with a Gold Medal for her work. She died at the age of 97, having changed the face of astronomy forever.

3 Start looking at one spot in the sky and scan for stars by slowly moving your head up and down. Make a map of the stars in your notebook.

4 If you hang around for a while, you'll notice that the stars seem to have moved. This is because the Earth is rotating!

5 If you are really lucky, you might spot a meteor shower! You will see pinpricks of light suddenly shoot across the sky and disappear. These 'shooting stars' last less than a second at a time. Each meteor shower is given a name – an online search will tell you when to look for one in your area.

A meteor is a piece of rock that burns up in the Earth's atmosphere (the gases that surround Earth) with a short streak of light. We call this a 'shooting star', even though it isn't a star!

23

Make invisible ink like JAMES JAY

Have you ever wanted to find a secret way to communicate with your friends? Well, that's exactly what a **PHYSICIAN** called James Jay did. Using his knowledge of chemistry, he invented invisible ink in 1775 so that he could write letters to his brother during a war!

Jay was born in 1732 in New York, USA, to a family of Huguenots, a group of French religious people, who ran away from France to find safety in North America. He had six brothers and sisters, including John Jay, one of the Founding Fathers of the USA.

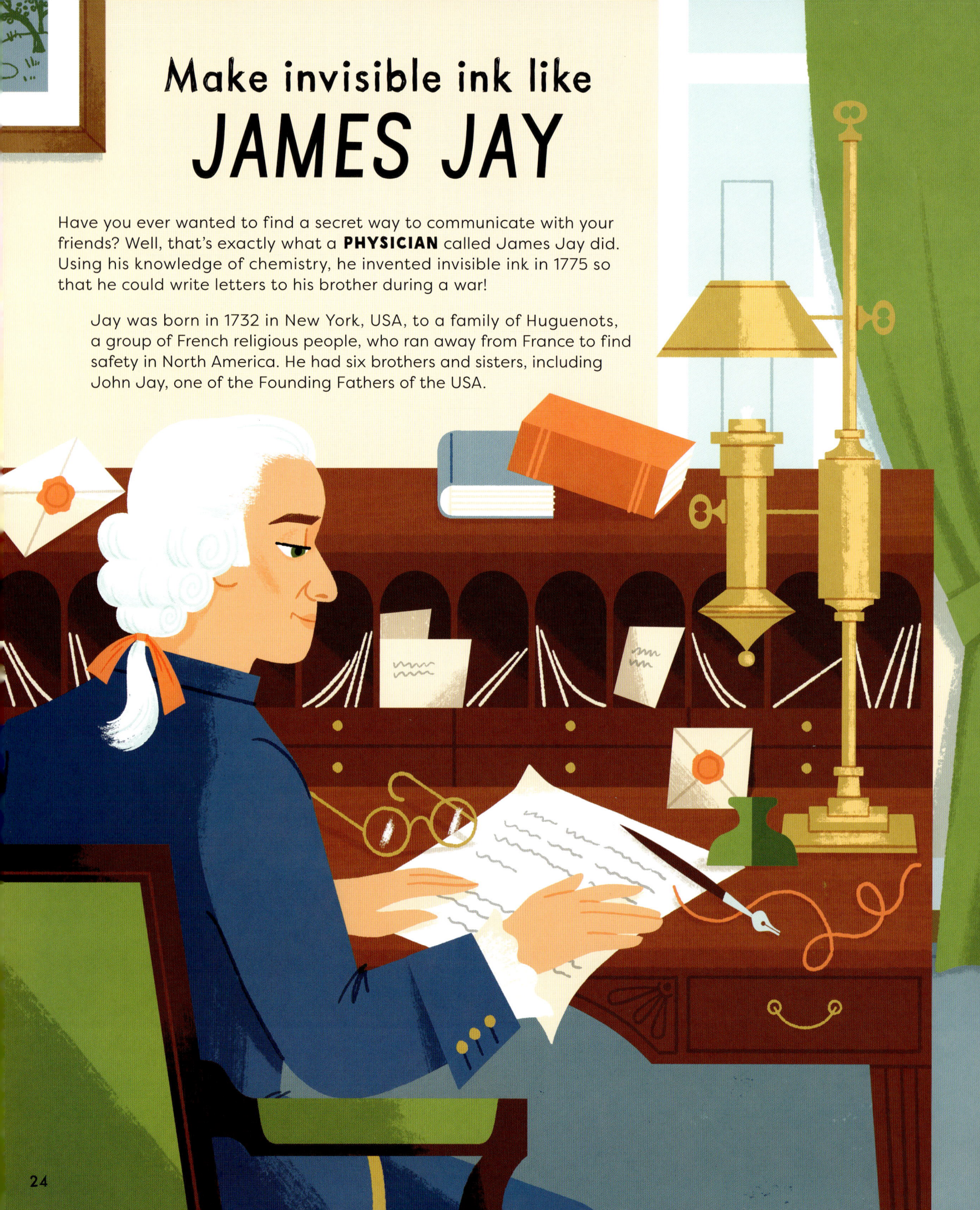

Jay created invisible ink so that he could send secret letters to his brother, John, during the American Revolutionary War. Jay would write some of the letters in normal ink and some in invisible ink. John would receive the letters and use a special 'decoding stain' to make the secret writing suddenly appear on the page!

Many invisible inks stay hidden until you brush another liquid on top, because the two liquids react together and change colour.

Using this invisible ink, Jay and John could talk freely about the war that was going on around them, without worrying that their letters would be stolen. Jay kept the recipe a secret, although he did allow some spy groups to use the ink too.

NOW IT'S YOUR TURN!

What you will need:

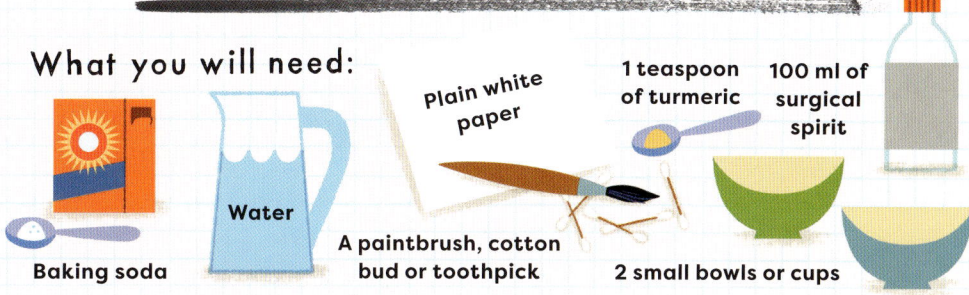

- Baking soda
- Water
- Plain white paper
- A paintbrush, cotton bud or toothpick
- 1 teaspoon of turmeric
- 100 ml of surgical spirit
- 2 small bowls or cups

1 Mix equal parts of baking soda and water to make your invisible ink.

2 Dip your paintbrush, cotton bud or toothpick into the ink and write a secret message on the white paper.

3 Allow it to dry.

4 In the second bowl, get an adult to help you mix the surgical spirit with the turmeric (see page 45 for safety tips).

5 Paint over the paper with the turmeric mixture to reveal your hidden message!

Explore evolution like
CHARLES DARWIN

Charles Darwin is famous for his theory of evolution, which is the idea that living things, including humans, have changed over millions of years to survive on our planet. He became an important **EVOLUTIONARY BIOLOGIST**.

Darwin was born in 1809 in Shropshire, UK. As a boy, he didn't do very well at school. His father wanted him to become a doctor, but Darwin didn't enjoy medical school, so instead he studied theology (religion) at the University of Cambridge, spending much of his time there learning about plants, animals and nature.

NOW IT'S YOUR TURN!

What you will need:

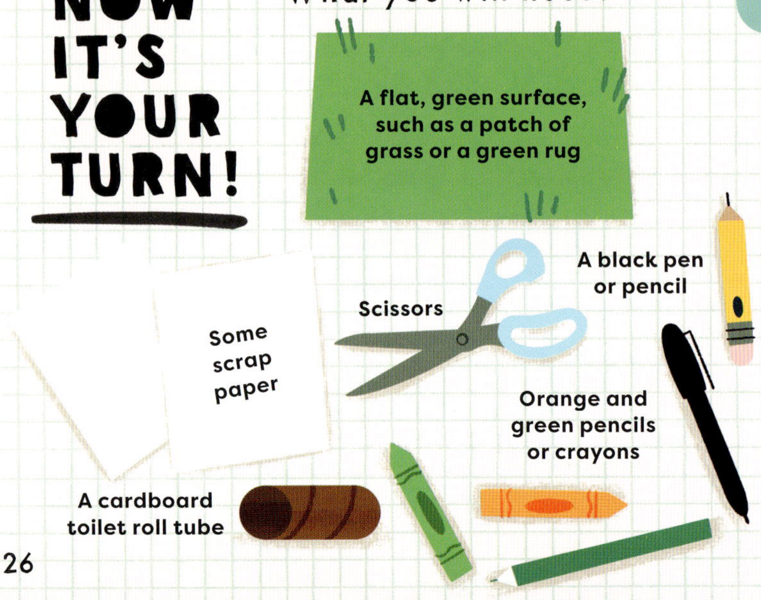

- A flat, green surface, such as a patch of grass or a green rug
- Some scrap paper
- Scissors
- A black pen or pencil
- Orange and green pencils or crayons
- A cardboard toilet roll tube

1 Place your toilet roll tube on the scrap paper and draw around it with your black pen or pencil to create a circle. Do this 15 times, then use the scissors to cut each circle out.

2 Colour 7 of your counters orange and 8 of your counters green. Then draw a beetle shape on top of each one with your black pen or pencil. Now you have 7 orange beetles and 8 green beetles!

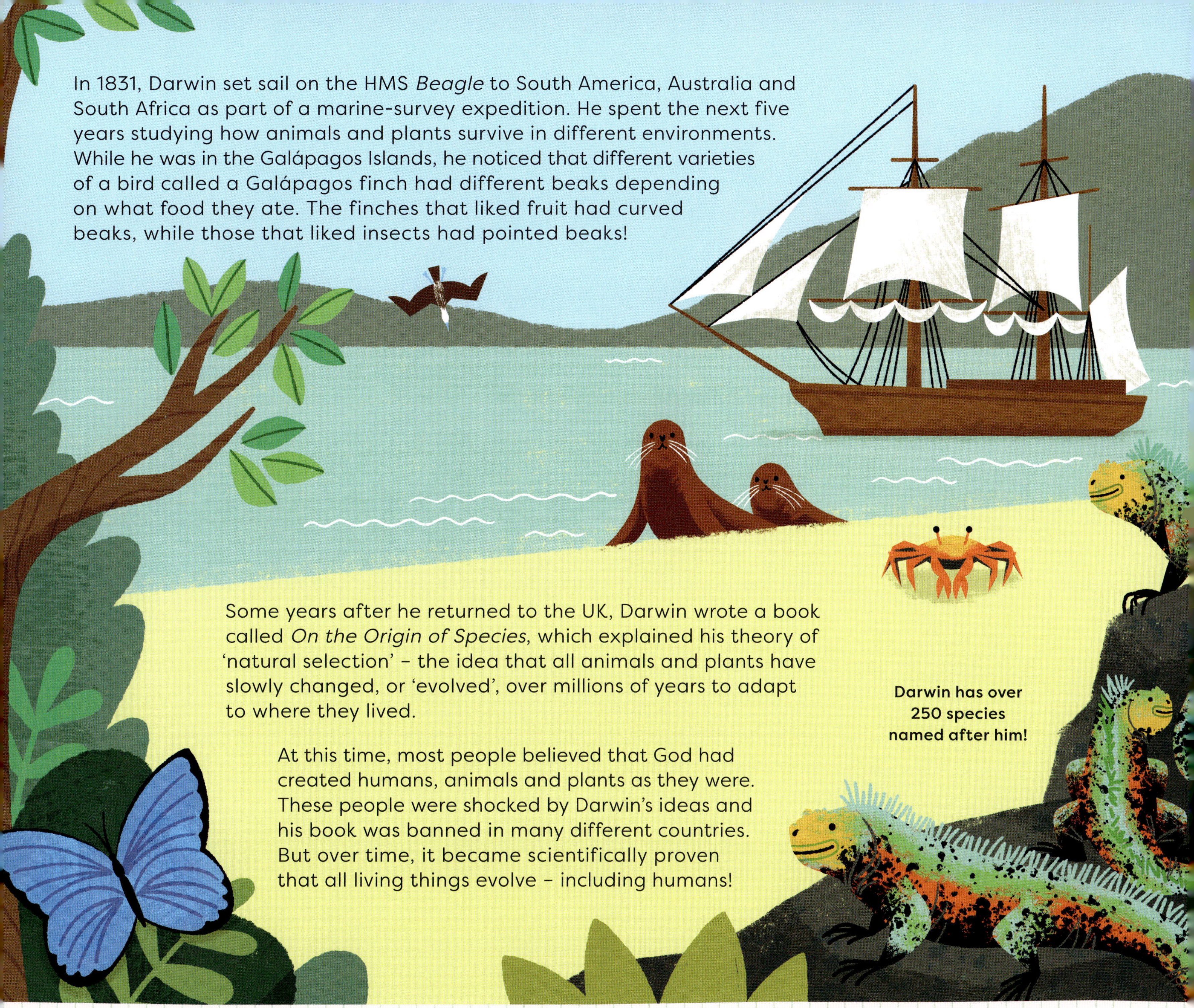

In 1831, Darwin set sail on the HMS *Beagle* to South America, Australia and South Africa as part of a marine-survey expedition. He spent the next five years studying how animals and plants survive in different environments. While he was in the Galápagos Islands, he noticed that different varieties of a bird called a Galápagos finch had different beaks depending on what food they ate. The finches that liked fruit had curved beaks, while those that liked insects had pointed beaks!

Some years after he returned to the UK, Darwin wrote a book called *On the Origin of Species*, which explained his theory of 'natural selection' – the idea that all animals and plants have slowly changed, or 'evolved', over millions of years to adapt to where they lived.

Darwin has over 250 species named after him!

At this time, most people believed that God had created humans, animals and plants as they were. These people were shocked by Darwin's ideas and his book was banned in many different countries. But over time, it became scientifically proven that all living things evolve – including humans!

3 Lay out 7 of the orange beetles on your green surface. This is your 'starting population' of beetles. Now add 1 green beetle. This beetle has a 'gene mutation', which made it a different colour to the rest.

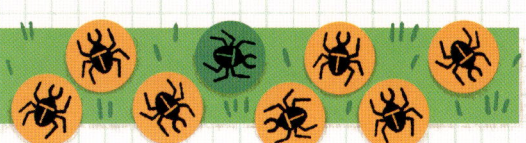

4 Imagine you are a predator, such as a bird. You, as a predator, will pretend to eat the beetles that stand out the most – so take away 4 of the orange beetles.

5 The beetles that are left have babies! Give each beetle a baby that looks like it. You will now have 6 orange beetles and 2 green beetles.

6 Repeat steps 4 and 5! How many orange and green beetles are there now?

7 The green beetles blend in with the grass background, so they are more likely to survive the predator! Over each repetition, the green beetles increase in number.

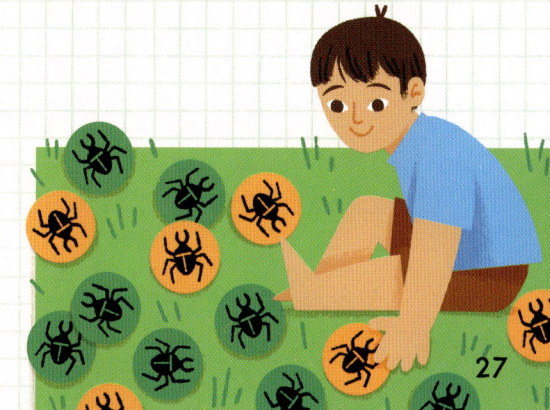

Search for fossils like
MARY ANNING

Mary Anning was born in 1799 in Lyme Regis, a small seaside town on the south coast of the UK. Anning was the 10th child to be born in her family and she had a stroke of luck as a baby when she survived a lightning strike, which killed three grown-ups!

Anning's family were very poor, so she would help her family hunt for shells and bones on the beach and sell them to tourists. When she was just 11, her father died, but Anning did not give up searching the beach for treasures.

One day, Anning's brother Joseph found the fossil skull of an enormous sea creature on the beach. A year later, Anning found the rest of the enormous prehistoric monster, which later became known as an *Ichthyosaur* – the first to ever be discovered. Several years later, Anning discovered the first complete *Plesiosaur*, and she also found the first fossil in Britain of a flying reptile called a *Pterosaur*!

NOW IT'S YOUR TURN!

What you will need:
* 250 g of plain flour
* 125 g of table salt
* 125 ml of water
* A rolling pin
* Some seashells
* A tray
* Paint brushes

1. Mix the flour and salt together in a bowl.
2. Add the water and mix everything together until a dough is formed.
3. Flatten the dough with a rolling pin or your hands.

At this time, people believed that women couldn't be scientists, but Anning taught herself geology and how to draw scientific illustrations, and she became an expert in fossil hunting.

Anning also found a lot of fossilised poo, known as 'coprolites', and used it to work out what sea creatures ate. Her discoveries helped start the study of ancient animal behaviour.

Anning died in 1847, but her work wasn't widely recognised until much later, mainly because Anning was a woman and came from a poor background. Some men even tried to claim Anning's work as their own. Nowadays, Anning is thought of as one of the most important people in **PALAEONTOLOGY** – the study of ancient life through fossils.

4 Press the shells into the dough to make fossil shapes. Once you've pressed the shell into the dough, very gently remove it to leave the imprint in the dough.

5 Leave the fossils to air dry, or get an adult to help you dry them gently in the oven.

6 You can then use them in a fossil dig! Place them in a tray and cover them with sand. Use brushes to search for your fossils. Can you trace them back to the shells that made them?

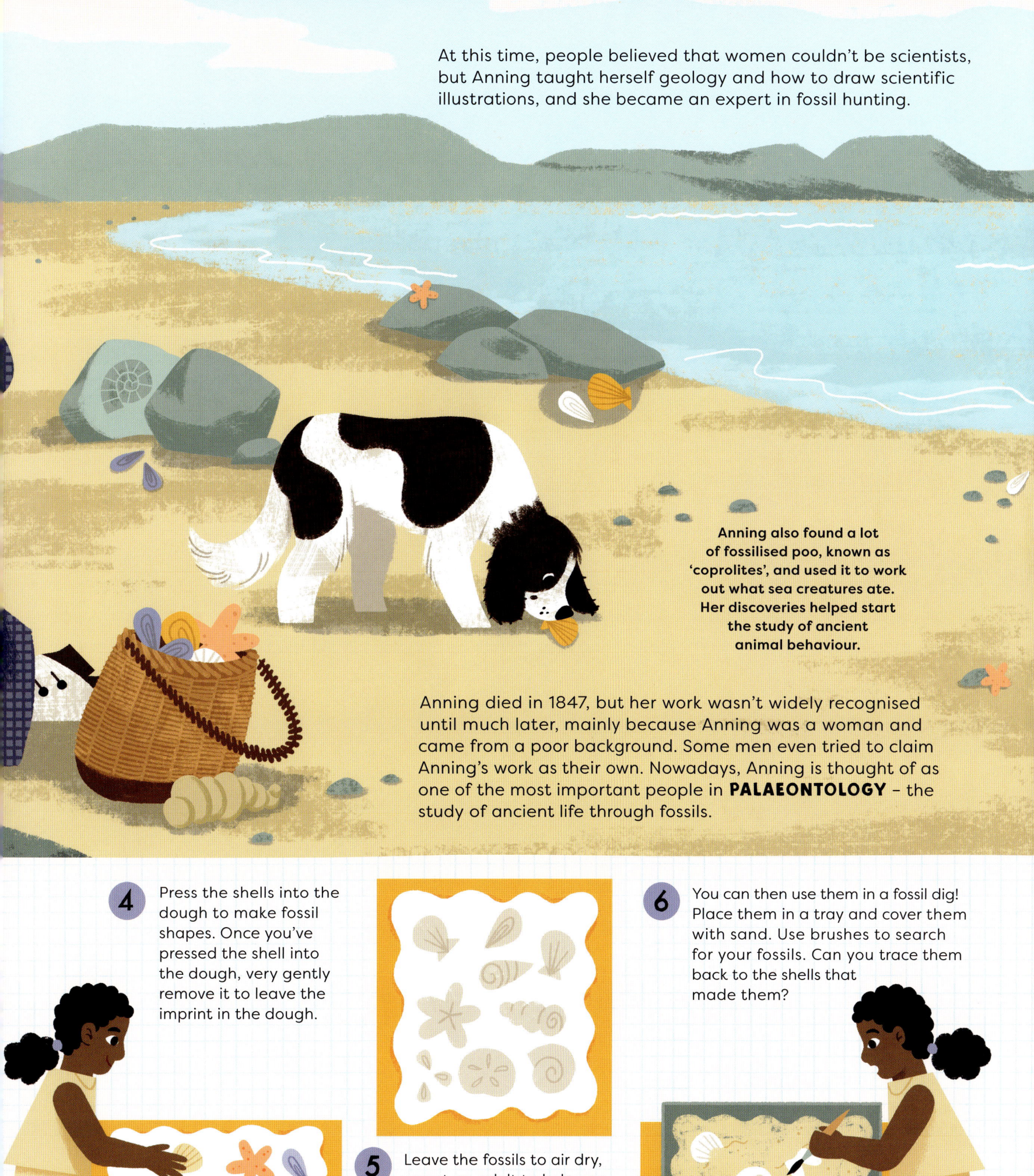

Make static electricity like NIKOLA TESLA

Nikola Tesla was born in 1856 in the Austrian Empire (now Croatia) to Serbian parents during an electrical storm, and he spent his life working on his passion: electricity!

While studying **ELECTRICAL ENGINEERING** at university, Tesla learnt about alternating current, which had been developed by Michael Faraday and Hippolyte Pixii.

A current is a flow of electricity. A direct current (DC) can only flow in one direction, but an alternating current (AC) allows the flow of electricity to change direction. It can travel larger distances and is safer to use than DC. Using his knowledge of electricity, Tesla helped to make AC even better and easier to use around the world.

Tesla's mother, Georgina-Djuka, came from a family of inventors. She built many different tools and handy instruments to be used around their home.

Tesla also invented the Tesla coil, a device that can spread electricity without wires. It does this by raising or lowering the voltage (how much pressure there is on the electrical current in a circuit) using AC electricity. Very high voltages can be very dangerous, but Tesla coils can make extremely high voltages in a way that is safer for humans to use.

In 1896, Tesla created an electrical power station that used energy from a famous group of waterfalls called Niagara Falls – something Tesla had dreamed of achieving since he was a child!

He died in 1943, leaving behind many ideas for scientific equipment in his notebooks, some of which are still secret inventions that haven't been built yet!

Tesla was a great entertainer and showman, and he often tried to make people think his science was magic.

NOW IT'S YOUR TURN!
▼▼▼▼▼▼▼

What you will need:
* A tap with running water
* A plastic comb or ruler
* A duster or a woolly jumper

1 Charge your plastic comb or ruler by rubbing it against the duster or woolly jumper.

2 Turn on your tap so you have a thin stream of slowly running water.

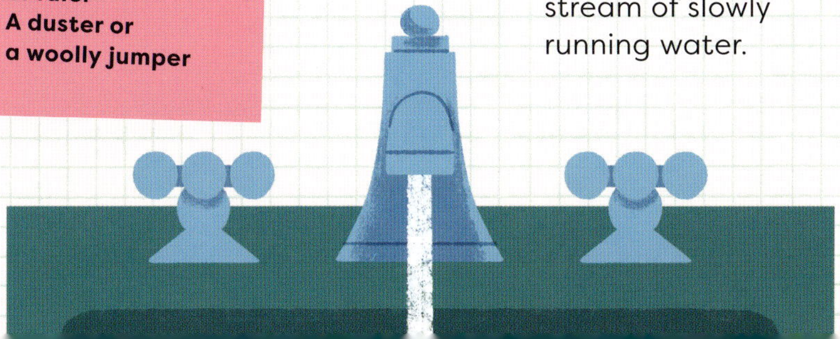

3 Bring your comb or ruler close to, but not touching, the stream of water.

4 Depending on whether your comb or ruler is charged negatively or positively, the water will bend towards it or away from it!

When you rub the comb or ruler, tiny bits called charges move around. If the plastic gains extra charges, it becomes negative. If it loses charges, it becomes positive.

Test acids and alkalines like
S. P. L. SØRENSEN

Søren Peder Lauritz Sørensen was a Danish **CHEMIST** who invented the pH scale to test how acidic or alkaline something is. An acid is a chemical substance that can make food taste tangy, sour or sweet. Lemon and vinegar contain acids. The opposite of an acid is an alkaline, and these can be found in things such as milk, soap and toothpaste.

Sørensen was born in 1868, in a small town near the coast of Denmark. He studied medicine, but was inspired to change to chemistry after meeting a Danish chemist called S. M. Jørgensen. Sørensen worked in the Carlsberg Laboratory, which was well known for discovering better ways to brew beer.

Sørensen's pH scale ranged from 0-14. While he was working for Carlsberg, Sørensen figured out that anything with a pH from 0 to 6 is an acid, anything from 8 to 14 is an alkaline, and anything in the middle, at pH 7, is neutral.

Today, over 100 years later, we still use Sørensen's pH scale for many different reasons, from testing batteries to checking the health of our oceans.

Neutral substances, such as water and blood, aren't acid or alkaline. If your blood doesn't test neutral, you might be ill, so the pH scale is a really useful way of checking your health.

NOW IT'S YOUR TURN!

1. Put the cabbage into the saucepan and fill it with water until the cabbage is covered.

2. Ask a grown-up to help you heat the saucepan and simmer the cabbage for 10 minutes.

What you will need:
* A large handful of chopped red cabbage
* A large saucepan
* Water
* A hob
* A colander or sieve
* A jug
* Paper cups or glasses
* Liquids to test (vinegar, lemon juice, fizzy water, milk, washing-up liquid, etc.)
* A teaspoon

3. Carefully sieve the purple cabbage liquid from the saucepan into a jug and leave to cool.

4. Pour small amounts of your chosen liquids into the cups.

5. Add three teaspoons of the purple cabbage liquid into the cups, one at a time.

6. If there is an acid in your cup and you add purple cabbage liquid, the purple cabbage liquid will turn red.

If you have an alkali, the liquid will turn from purple to green!

If the purple doesn't change colour – what do you think you have? (Hint, if it isn't an acid or an alkali what could it be?)

TIP: If you have any purple liquid left in your jug when you've finished, grab a paper straw and blow bubbles into the cabbage liquid. The purple liquid should turn red. Why do you think that is?

Collect plants like YNÉS MEXÍA

You might think you have to start young to be successful, but Ynés Enriquetta Julietta Mexía was 55 years old when she became a **BOTANIST**. By the time she died, she had spent over 13 years travelling around, collecting and cataloguing plants.

Mexía was born in 1870 in Washington DC, USA, and her family moved around a lot. Mexía spent much of her childhood outdoors, exploring and learning. She moved to Mexico as a teenager to help her father on his ranch and looked after it for 30 years after he died.

By becoming friends with the local people she met on her trips, and valuing their expertise, Mexía became a very popular botanist.

When Mexía moved back to the USA, she became passionate about conservation and saving the California Redwood forests. She went to university aged 51 to study science and natural history, which was very unusual for a woman of her age back then. During her first trip cataloguing and categorising plants, she gathered over 1,500 specimens!

Mexía was often alone for months at a time, with only a horse for company! Some of the places she visited were dangerous and she braved earthquakes, bogs and poisonous berries, all so that she could find new plants and flowers.

NOW IT'S YOUR TURN!

What you will need:

1. Carefully collect a small section of the plant you are interested in. Don't forget to ask permission from whoever owns the flowers.

2. Place a sheet of newspaper or rough paper between the pages of a heavy book.

3. Place your plant on the newspaper or rough paper and close the book.

4. Layer more books on top of the book with the plant in it. Store this book pile for a week. Keep it somewhere warm.

5. Once your plant is dry, remove it from the book.

6. Use PVA glue or sticky tape to stick your plant onto card or paper.

7. Write down details and information about the plant you have collected. Don't forget to include the name of the plant, when it was collected and who found it.

TIP: Be sensitive to nature! There is a code of good behaviour when you are picking or collecting plants. Don't pick too many, collect carefully and leave enough for the plant to survive. And always make sure you can identify the flower before you pick it!

By the end of her life, Mexía had collected over 145,000 plants, categorised over 500 for the first time and even had some named after her. Mexía's contribution to botany is so valuable that her collections are still being used today!

Measure the speed of light like
ALBERT EINSTEIN

Albert Einstein became a world-famous **PHYSICIST**. He was born in Germany in 1879 to a Jewish family. Einstein didn't do very well in school, but he loved maths and puzzles. He was fascinated by the compass his father gave him when he was five – Einstein wanted to know why the magnetic needle always pointed north.

By 16, Einstein had written a scientific paper and got a place at university to study physics and maths. He wanted to become a teacher, but no one would give him a job, so he ended up working at a patent office in Switzerland, where he recorded other people's inventions and developed some of his own, too.

Einstein shared his ideas about energy and mass with the world when he was 26. He believed that anything we see and touch can be turned into energy. His famous equation $E = mc^2$ explained how mass, which is related to how heavy something is, can be turned into energy. Energy (E) equals the mass (m) of something multiplied by the speed of light (c) multiplied by the speed of light again (^{2}).

NOW IT'S YOUR TURN!

What you will need:
* A bar of chocolate
* A microwave
* A ruler
* A calculator
* A microwaveable plate

1. Remove the turntable from the microwave. Place your chocolate bar on the plate and put it in the microwave.

2. Run the microwave for about 10 seconds. Carefully remove the plate and check whether there are any melted spots of chocolate.

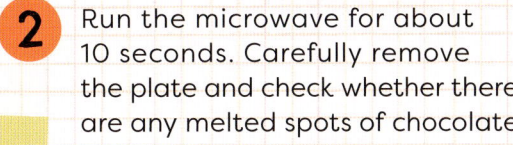

3. Repeat in 10-second bursts until melted spots appear. Make sure you don't overdo it and burn the chocolate!

4. Carefully use a ruler to measure the distance in centimetres between 2 melted spots that are next to each other.

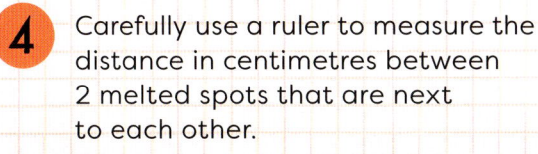

5. Multiply the distance by 2. This gives you the wavelength of light!

6. Check what frequency your microwave runs at. A standard frequency is 2.45 gigahertz. Multiply the wavelength in centimetres by the frequency in hertz, so if your microwave runs at 2.45 gigahertz, you multiply the wavelength by 2,450,000,000.

7. This gives you the answer in centimetres per second, but you need it in metres per second, so divide your answer by 100. The actual speed of light is 299,792,458 metres per second. What did you get? How accurate was your experiment? You may now eat the chocolate!

TIP: To work out c (the speed of light) you need to multiply the wavelength by the frequency of the microwave. Wavelength is the distance between two peaks in the wave of light. Frequency is how many times the light waves move up and down per second.

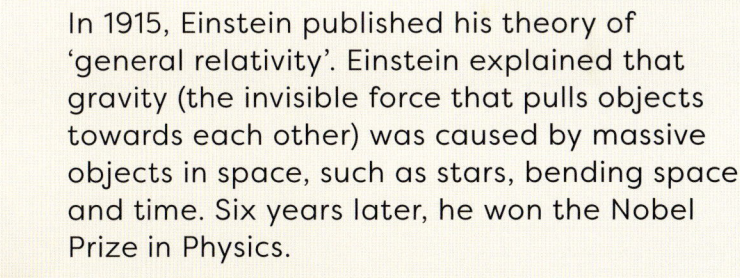

In 1915, Einstein published his theory of 'general relativity'. Einstein explained that gravity (the invisible force that pulls objects towards each other) was caused by massive objects in space, such as stars, bending space and time. Six years later, he won the Nobel Prize in Physics.

Sadly, in the 1930s, Einstein was forced to leave his country. The Nazis had taken control of Germany and wanted to get rid of all Jewish people. He escaped to the USA where he worked on his theories for the rest of his life. Einstein had changed how we understand space and the universe forever!

Einstein was able to show that as objects approach the speed of light, distances squash and time actually stretches!

Grow mould like
ALEXANDER FLEMING

Alexander Fleming was a **MICROBIOLOGIST** who made some incredible, life-saving discoveries . . . by mistake! Fleming was born in Scotland in 1881 to a big farming family. He studied medicine and came top of his class at university, but rather than becoming a doctor, he decided to become a scientist, studying tiny organisms called bacteria.

During the First World War, Fleming went with the Army Medical Corps to France, researching better ways to treat wounds and infections. At this time, people would often die from cuts and scratches that became infected. Fleming found that a mixture of salt and water could safely clean large wounds.

After the war, Fleming returned to his laboratory. One day, when he had a cold, his snot dripped onto some bacteria. After a few weeks he noticed that the bacteria were slowly dying away! It made him realise that mucus (snot) has a small amount of natural antiseptic in it, which means it can stop diseases from spreading.

In 1928, Fleming made an even more incredible accidental discovery. He went on holiday and forgot to clear away some dishes in his lab, which contained a bacteria called *Staphylococcus*. When he returned, Fleming realised that one of the dishes had been contaminated and had mould all over it. Studying the dish further, he discovered that the mould had killed off some of the bacteria. Fleming had accidentally discovered penicillin, the world's first antibiotic!

NOW IT'S YOUR TURN!

What you will need:

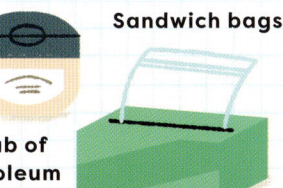
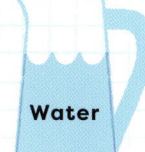

5 slices of white bread
A tub of petroleum jelly
Sandwich bags
Water
Vinegar

1. Keep one piece of bread as it is. Cover one in petroleum jelly. Sprinkle vinegar over one. Sprinkle the fourth and fifth with water.

2. Carefully put one of the water-soaked pieces into a sandwich bag and seal it. Put the sandwich bag in the fridge.

3. Put the other pieces of bread somewhere warm and out of the way, such as in a kitchen cupboard, or on a windowsill.

4. Leave the bread for a week, then go back and see which pieces have mould on them. Why do you think those ones had the most mould? Why might others have grown less mould?

5. Make sure you throw the mouldy bread in the bin and wash your hands!

TIP: You can try different preservatives and different mould-growing conditions.

Penicillin is still used around the world to treat all sorts of infections – from meningitis to ear infections.

Blend oil like ALICE BALL

Alice Ball was a **CHEMIST** who, at the age of just 23, found a cure for a disease called leprosy. Ball was born in 1892 in Seattle, USA, to a family of successful photographers. She studied chemistry and pharmacy at the University of Washington, before winning a scholarship to the University of Hawaii, where Ball became the first Black student and the first woman to graduate from the university.

At this time, a disease called leprosy (also known as Hansen's disease) was spreading in the USA. It caused painful growths on the skin, numbness, and damage to the nerves and eyes. To stop the disease spreading, police arrested anyone who had leprosy and forced them to live on the island of Molokaʻi, Hawaii, where they were often separated from their families.

Scientists already knew that the oil of the chaulmoogra tree could be used to treat leprosy, but no one could figure out how to turn it into a medicine. It was too painful to swallow or inject the oil by itself. After a lot of experimentation, Ball found a way to separate the oil and blend it with water so it could be safely used in an injection. This new treatment finally helped people to recover from leprosy, allowing them to return to their families!

Tragically, Ball died the following year, aged 24, before she had the chance to publish her findings. Other people took credit for her discoveries, and it wasn't until 2000 that the process that Ball developed to fight leprosy was finally formally named 'the Ball Method'. Her treatments transformed many people's lives.

NOW IT'S YOUR TURN!

What you will need:

- 3 large oranges
- A mason jar or jam jar
- A sieve or strainer
- Paper towels
- Olive oil
- A rolling pin or pestle and mortar or food processor
- A small bowl

1 Wash and dry the oranges before peeling them. Try to remove any of the white bits (pith) from the peel.

2 Leave the peels on a paper towel and allow to dry for a few days. Don't throw away the rest of the fruit – you can eat it!

3 When the peels are dry, find an adult to help you, and grind the peels using a pestle and mortar or food processor, or bash them down with a rolling pin! Put the peels into a jar.

4 Carefully pour some olive oil into the jar, until all the peels are covered.

5 Put the lid on the jar tightly and shake! Then leave the jar as it is for a week. You can shake it now and again.

6 Strain the liquid from the jar into a bowl, using a sieve or strainer. Squeeze the peels out so more liquid is released into the bowl.

7 The liquid left in the bowl is your orange oil!

Make crystals like DOROTHY HODGKIN

Dorothy Hodgkin was a British chemist who had a special skill: making crystals! Hodgkin became a pioneering **CRYSTALLOGRAPHER**. She was born in 1910 in Egypt, where her parents worked as archaeologists. Hodgkin and her younger sisters were sent to school in the UK, but they returned to Egypt during the holidays to join their parents on digs.

NOW IT'S YOUR TURN!

What you will need:
* Water
* A kettle
* A pencil
* Table salt
* A piece of string
* A jar or container
* A paperclip

1. Boil water in a kettle and let it cool for at least 10 minutes. Ask a grown-up to help you carefully pour warm water into the container until it's about three-quarters full.

2. Add salt, one tablespoon at a time. Let it dissolve before you add the next spoonful. Stop when no more salt dissolves and it collects at the bottom of the container.

3. Tie one end of the string around the pencil and tie the other end around the paperclip.

When she was 10 years old, Hodgkin became interested in crystals and chemistry. She had to fight to study science with the boys at school, but she went on to become the third woman ever to earn a high-class degree in chemistry at the University of Oxford. It was here that she started learning about the structure of crystals, and how to photograph them using X-rays. X-ray diffraction is a way of seeing how the tiny crystal molecules are arranged.

After beginning research at the University of Cambridge, Hodgkin went on to become a chemistry teacher and researcher. Alexander Fleming had recently discovered penicillin (see page 38), but chemists needed to know more about the structure of penicillin to create large batches of the medicine. It took Hodgkin four years to crack the code!

Hodgkin also found the structure of insulin and vitamin B12, which has the most complicated structure of all the vitamins. With her work, medicines to help people with diabetes were hugely improved.

Hodgkin was awarded the Nobel Prize in Chemistry in 1964, and she is still the only British woman to have won a Nobel Prize in science. She died at the age of 84, and will forever be remembered for her groundbreaking discoveries.

4. Dangle the paperclip into the water, but don't let it touch the sides or the bottom of the container. Adjust the string length by wrapping it around the pencil.

5. Rest the pencil on the top of the container so the paperclip stays in place.

6. Leave the experiment for one week and you should see salt crystals start to form on the string!

TIP: You can do this experiment with sugar too!

Extract DNA like ROSALIND FRANKLIN

Rosalind Franklin was an incredible chemist who helped the world understand DNA, the chemical code inside all of us that tells our bodies what we will look like and how we might behave. Her work has been very important to the scientific field of **GENETICS**.

Franklin was born in 1920 to a Jewish family in London, UK, and she studied chemistry at the University of Cambridge. When the Second World War began, Franklin researched the structures of coal and carbon to help people design charcoal filters for gas masks in the UK.

After the war, Franklin learned to use X-rays to study objects and find out what they are made of. This new technique was called X-ray crystallography. At this time, many scientists were trying to discover what DNA looks like, and Franklin used X-ray crystallography to find out. With the help of Raymond Gosling, her student, Franklin took pictures of DNA. They were able to show that there were not one, but two forms of DNA, and that it looked like a long, twisted rope ladder, known as a 'double helix'. This was a big breakthrough – it meant that scientists could finally start decoding DNA.

Today, DNA tests are very useful for tracking family histories, diagnosing certain diseases and solving crimes.

But before Franklin's work was formally recognised, two other scientists, James Watson and Francis Crick, used Franklin's photo and some of her research to prove that DNA had a double helix. Sadly, Franklin was not credited for her work, and she died very soon after from cancer, aged just 37.

Watson and Crick, along with Franklin's colleague Maurice Wilkins, went on to win the Nobel Prize in 1962. Because she died so early, it is hard to say whether Franklin would have won her own Nobel Prize. Today, she is finally celebrated for her incredible scientific work which changed the world forever.

NOW IT'S YOUR TURN!

1. Put the strawberries into the sandwich bag and seal.

2. Squash the fruit into a smooth pulp by pressing through the bag.

What you will need:
* 2 strawberries
* A sealable sandwich bag
* Warm water
* 2 clear cups or beakers
* 4 teaspoons of salt
* 2 teaspoons of washing-up liquid
* A colander or sieve
* A measuring jug
* A coffee filter or paper towel
* Black paper, card or cloth
* 120 ml of surgical spirit
* Tweezers (optional)

3. Add warm water to one of the clear cups or beakers until it is half full, then stir in the salt until it dissolves. Add the washing-up liquid and stir.

4. Add this mixture to the plastic bag and reseal, then mix into the fruit by pressing through the bag. Do this for 10 minutes.

5. Place the sieve on top of the jug. Place the coffee filter or paper towel into the sieve. Pour the liquid from the bag through the sieve so it filters into the jug. This may take some time.

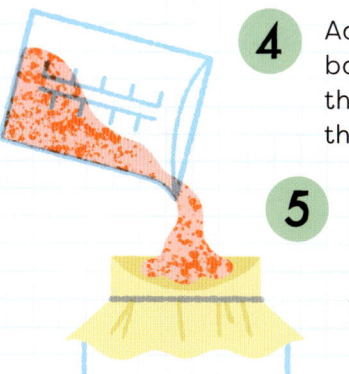

6. Pour the drained liquid from the jug into the other cup or beaker and place the cup or beaker onto your black paper.

7. Ask a grown-up to help you add the surgical spirit by carefully pouring it down the side of the cup or beaker. Do not mix or stir.

8. Slowly, white strands will start to form in the liquid at the top of the cup. This is your strawberry DNA! You can inspect it closer by hooking it out with tweezers.

9. You can try this again but with some of your own saliva to see your DNA!

TIP: Warning! Surgical spirit is used as an antiseptic to kill germs, but it can catch fire easily and it is very poisonous if you drink it. Only use it with the help of a grown-up, in a well-ventilated room.

Measure your heartbeat like
MARIE MAYNARD DALY

Marie Maynard Daly was a brilliant **BIOCHEMIST**, and the first Black woman to get a PhD in chemistry in the USA. Her groundbreaking research into heart health has changed the way people around the world eat, exercise and look after their bodies.

Daly was born in 1921 in New York, USA. Her father loved science and had started studying chemistry at university. Sadly, he had to drop out when he ran out of money. Daly was inspired by her father to study chemistry and she went on to complete her PhD at Columbia University. With the help of her tutor, Mary L. Caldwell, Daly researched how different chemicals in the body help us digest food.

While Daly was teaching and working as a chemist, she became interested in how a substance called 'cholesterol' affects the body. Cholesterol helps us make some of the vitamins and chemicals that keep us healthy, but Daly and another chemist called Quentin Deming were among the first to realise that too much cholesterol can be bad for your heart. Cholesterol can clog up your arteries, which makes it difficult for your heart to pump blood around the body and can lead to heart attacks.

Using her research, Daly was able to tell people about the importance of healthy eating and exercise for heart health.

In 1960, Daly became a professor at the Albert Einstein College of Medicine. After her father died, she created a scholarship fund in his memory for Black students who wanted to study chemistry at Queens College.

NOW IT'S YOUR TURN!

What you will need:
* A stopwatch, clock or timer
* A pen
* Some scrap paper

1 Find your pulse by placing your index finger (the finger next to your thumb) and middle finger on the inside of your wrist.

2 Count how many times you feel your pulse for 30 seconds. Multiply this number by 2 to get your resting pulse rate per minute. Write the number down.

3 Do star jumps or jog on the spot for 2 minutes.

4 Immediately measure your pulse rate again.

5 Rest for 1 minute and then measure your pulse rate.

6 Rest for 2 more minutes and then measure your pulse rate.

7 Repeat step 6 and then measure your pulse rate.

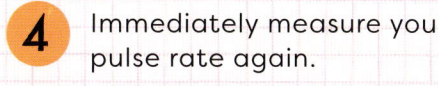

TIP: You can keep going until your pulse is back to the resting pulse rate.

8 Is your pulse back to its resting rate? How long does it take you to recover?

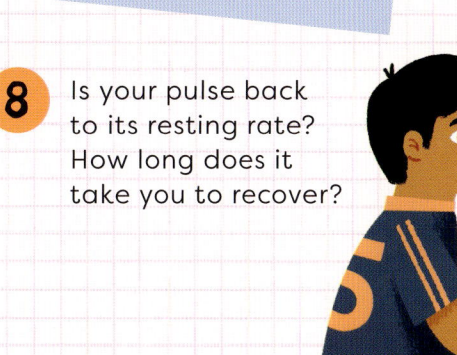

Make a crater like EUGENE MERLE SHOEMAKER

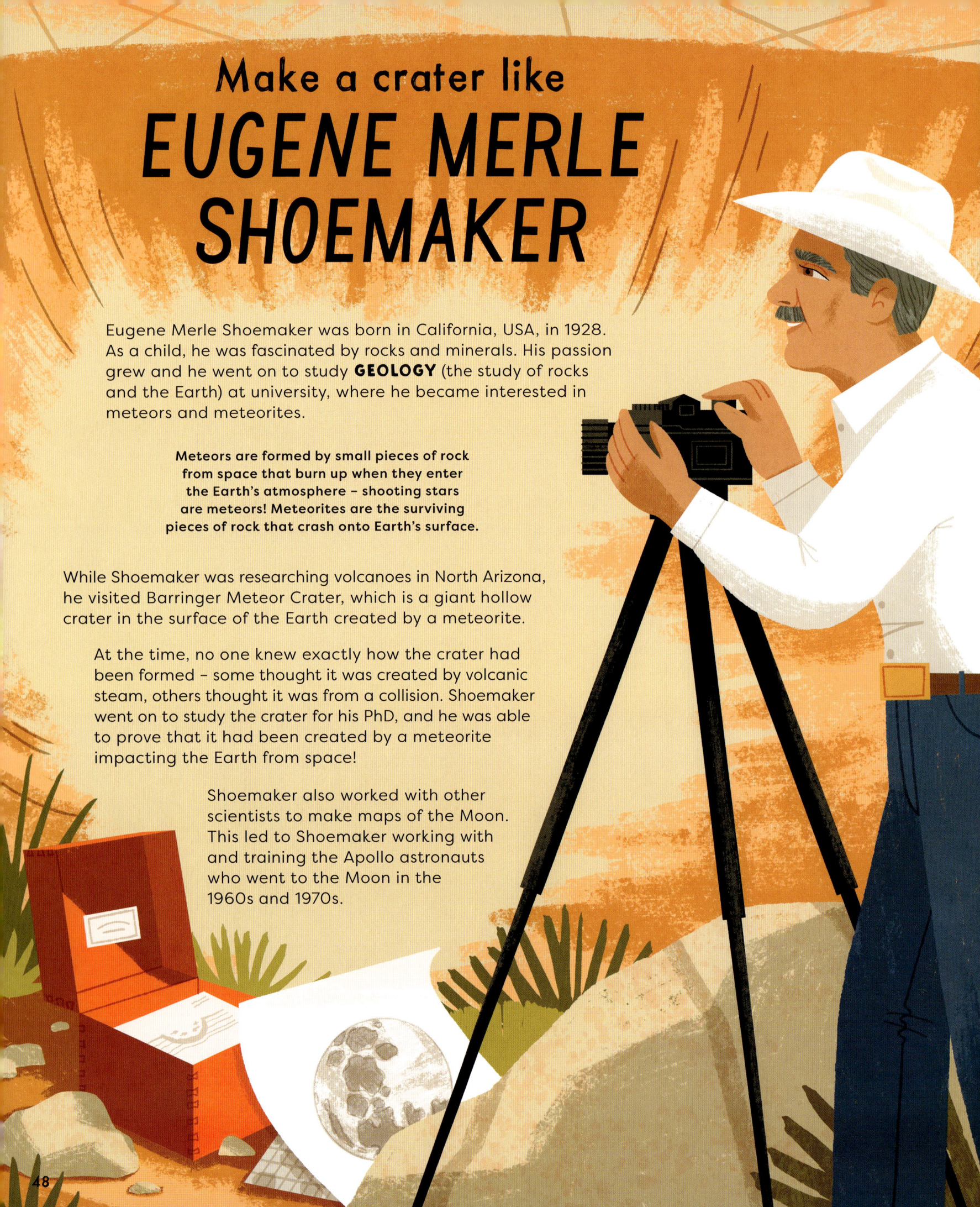

Eugene Merle Shoemaker was born in California, USA, in 1928. As a child, he was fascinated by rocks and minerals. His passion grew and he went on to study **GEOLOGY** (the study of rocks and the Earth) at university, where he became interested in meteors and meteorites.

Meteors are formed by small pieces of rock from space that burn up when they enter the Earth's atmosphere – shooting stars are meteors! Meteorites are the surviving pieces of rock that crash onto Earth's surface.

While Shoemaker was researching volcanoes in North Arizona, he visited Barringer Meteor Crater, which is a giant hollow crater in the surface of the Earth created by a meteorite.

At the time, no one knew exactly how the crater had been formed – some thought it was created by volcanic steam, others thought it was from a collision. Shoemaker went on to study the crater for his PhD, and he was able to prove that it had been created by a meteorite impacting the Earth from space!

Shoemaker also worked with other scientists to make maps of the Moon. This led to Shoemaker working with and training the Apollo astronauts who went to the Moon in the 1960s and 1970s.

Along with his wife, Carolyn Shoemaker (who was a fantastic asteroid hunter and astronomer too), and David Levy (an amateur astronomer), Shoemaker found a comet that was orbiting the planet Jupiter. Comet Shoemaker-Levy 9 collided with Jupiter in 1994 leaving a 'scar' that lasted for many months!

Shoemaker became an expert in finding impact craters all around the world. When he died, some of his ashes were flown to the Moon, where they still lie in a crater near the Moon's South Pole.

NOW IT'S YOUR TURN!

What you will need:

- A wide and shallow baking dish or tray, or a cardboard box
- Plain white flour
- Cocoa powder
- A sieve
- Marbles or other small balls

1. Add a layer of flour (about three centimetres thick) to cover the whole base of the dish, tray or box.

2. Sprinkle a layer of cocoa powder over the flour, using the sieve to apply it thinly and evenly.

3. Stand next to the tray and drop a marble or small ball into the tray from about a metre above.

4. Look closely at the impact crater that you've made. How far did the cocoa and flour spread? What colour is the surface around the collision site, and how does this compare to the surface elsewhere on the tray?

5. Experiment with different marbles and balls, and try dropping them from different heights. Do bigger balls make bigger impact craters?

Communicate with chimpanzees like
JANE GOODALL

Jane Goodall was a British **ETHOLOGIST**, which means someone who studies animal behaviour. She was born in 1934 and loved animals from a very early age, especially chimpanzees – her favourite toy was a chimp called Jubilee. Goodall dreamed of living in Africa and when she left school, she worked as a waitress until she had saved up enough money to board a ship to Kenya.

In Kenya, Goodall met Louis Leakey, a scientist who was looking for a researcher with enough patience to study chimpanzees in the wild.

Goodall jumped at the chance, and she set up a camp in the Gombe Stream Game Reserve in Tanzania to observe the chimps. It took her many months of working with them to build their trust.

NOW IT'S YOUR TURN!

What you will need: A partner, and the 6 chimp facial expression pictures shown below

1. Relaxed

2. Obedient

3. Excited

4. Distressed

5. Playful

6. Fearful

1 Pick a chimp facial expression from the pictures. Face your partner.

Over time, Goodall realised that the chimps had their own emotions, thoughts and personalities, just like humans. She also noticed that they could make and use tools, something that scientists thought only humans could do. Goodall began communicating with the chimps by making sounds, calls and facial expressions.

Instead of numbering them like the other scientists did, Goodall gave the chimps names. Her favourite was called David Greybeard, named after his grey beard!

Goodall went on to study the behaviour of chimpanzees at the University of Cambridge. She also started campaigning to protect jungles and the wildlife found within them. She became an inspiring activist, speaking out about climate change and conserving biodiversity. Goodall received many awards, including an honour called a DBE from the Queen, and the 2022 Stephen Hawking Medal for Science Communication.

2 Make the same expression as the chimp in the picture and see if your partner can work out what emotion you are showing.

3 If they get it right, then it is your partner's turn.

4 Do you make the same facial expressions when you feel these emotions?

Watch a volcano erupt like
KATIA KRAFFT

Katia Krafft was born in France in 1942. As a child, she loved sketching rock formations and was fascinated by volcanoes. Krafft went on to study physics and geochemistry at Strasbourg University, where she met another student called Maurice who shared her love of volcanoes. They got married and spent their honeymoon in Stromboli, Italy, filming a volcano up close. This was the start of their careers as **VOLCANOLOGISTS**, travelling the world to study and document volcanic eruptions.

Krafft was fearless! She wore special protective clothing and got as close to the eruptions as she could to film the bubbling lava and take samples of toxic fumes. Krafft wanted to show the world the beauty and power of volcanoes. But she also wanted to find out how harmful they could be. By taking many measurements and photos, she studied how creatures, plants and soil were affected by the volcanic ash and acid rain that fell after an eruption.

NOW IT'S YOUR TURN!

What you will need:

- Paintbrushes
- Paint (green, red and black)
- A teaspoon
- A plastic bottle
- 200 ml of vinegar
- Scissors
- A paper plate
- 2 A3 sheets of card
- Washing-up liquid
- Sticky tape
- Red food colouring
- 3 teaspoons of bicarbonate of soda

1. Place your bottle upside down in the middle of one of the sheets of card and draw around it to create a circle shape.

2. Cut a straight line through the card to the middle of the circle and cut the circle out.

3. Make a cone shape with the card, overlapping the edges, then tape it together, leaving a hole where you cut out the circle at the top. Cut around the bottom of the cone so that it sits flat.

Katia and Maurice Krafft were often the first people to arrive at an eruption, filming as much as they could. Their close-up photos and videos were unlike any the world had ever seen.

The Kraffts' films taught people around the world how to detect eruptions sooner. When a volcano in the Philippines began to show signs of an eruption, their video of another eruption in Colombia persuaded the president to evacuate people from the area, which saved thousands of lives.

In 1991, Katia and Maurice Krafft were filming with 41 other people at Mount Unzen in Japan when disaster struck. They got stuck in a pyroclastic flow, which is a flowing cloud of burning gas and ash that moves faster than a speeding car and is 10 times hotter than boiling water. Tragically, everyone died.

Today, the Kraffts' work is honoured in various documentaries, medals and even a volcanic crater, the M and K Krafft Crater, in Réunion, France.

4 Place the paper cone over the bottle. Tape the top of the cone to the top of the bottle to hold it in place. Tape the base of the cone to the other sheet of card.

5 Paint the cone to make it look like a volcano, then leave it to dry.

6 Fill two-thirds of your bottle with water. Add three teaspoons of bicarbonate of soda into the bottle and stir until it dissolves.

7 Add a few drops of food colouring to make it look like lava.

8 Add a generous squirt of washing up liquid.

9 Quickly pour in the vinegar and watch your eruption!

Design an aeroplane like
CHRISTINE DARDEN

Christine Darden is an **AERONAUTICAL ENGINEER** who worked at NASA for over 40 years! She is known around the world for her important work investigating supersonic aircraft noise, as well as helping the first astronauts land on the Moon!

Darden was born in 1942 in North Carolina, USA. As a child, she enjoyed finding out how things worked – like taking apart and fixing her own bicycle – and she worked hard in school, finishing top of her class. Darden studied maths at Hampton University, a private university for Black students. At this time, Black people were not treated equally to white people, and Darden took part in many peaceful protests at her university, campaigning for equality.

In 1967, Darden got a job at NASA as a 'human computer'. This was a time when the machines we know as computers were still in the early stages of development. A group of talented female mathematicians would do calculations by hand, then pass these on to the engineers, in order to research rockets and plane flights.

The work Darden and the other human computers did was essential for NASA, but it was usually the male engineers who got all the credit and made all the money. Darden bravely spoke out about how unfair this was and soon after, she became one of the first Black woman to be made an engineer at NASA.

A supersonic jet is an aeroplane that can travel faster than the speed of sound. It moves so quickly that it creates a sonic boom, which is a very, very loud noise!

Darden's aeronautical research contributed to some incredibly clever plane designs, including a supersonic jet! She worked on designs that made these super-fast jet planes less noisy and wrote lots of scientific papers. Darden eventually retired in 2007. She's since been awarded countless medals and awards and spends her retirement giving inspirational talks across the USA.

NOW IT'S YOUR TURN!

What you will need:
* A sheet of A4 paper

1 Start with your piece of paper sitting in portrait position.

2 Fold the left half to the right half in order to create a crease that runs down the centre, then unfold.

3 Fold the top left corner down to the centre. Repeat with the top right corner.

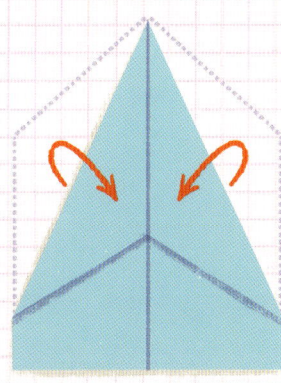

4 Fold the new left corner (which is about half way down the paper now) into the centre.

5 Repeat with the new right corner.

6 Fold the plane in half so the folds are on the outside.

7 Fold the left edge down to the right to form one wing.

8 Turn the plane over.

9 Fold the right edge down to the left to form the other wing.

10 Run your nail down the edges to make the wings crisp and the nose tip pointy!

11 Unfold the wings until they're level.

12 Hold the body and throw your plane!

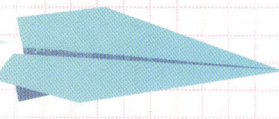

Study black holes like
STEPHEN HAWKING

Stephen Hawking was a British physicist and mathematician, famous for his groundbreaking work on black holes. Black holes are the remains of massive stars that explode when they die, creating a place where gravity pulls so much that not even light can escape.

Hawking was born during the Second World War in 1942. His whole family loved learning and they would spend hours together, each with their nose in a book. Hawking found it difficult to focus at school, but he was particularly interested in maths and physics, and he enjoyed lying outside at night, gazing at the stars.

After studying physics and chemistry, Hawking went to the University of Cambridge to study **COSMOLOGY** – the study of how the universe was created and how it might end.

However, aged just 21, Hawking received some terrible news. Doctors told him he had a disease called ALS, which would gradually stop him from being able to move and speak. They believed he might only have two years to live.

Hawking was devastated by his diagnosis, but he worked harder than ever, getting his PhD and continuing his research as a professor. Hawking was fascinated by black holes and spent a lot of his time doing complicated calculations to figure out how they are created.

Eventually, Stephen lost his ability to talk or move. He communicated using a special talking device, which he controlled by moving muscles in his face, and he used a wheelchair to get around. He loved dancing in his wheelchair at parties and driving it a little *too* fast around Cambridge!

Hawking's book *A Brief History of Time: From the Big Bang to Black Holes*, published in 1988, has now sold more than 10 million copies!

Hawking changed how people around the world thought about the universe. By the time he died in 2018, at the age of 76, he had written many books, appeared on lots of TV shows and won countless prizes and medals.

NOW IT'S YOUR TURN!

1 If you are using an elastic bandage or an old pair of tights, cut it into a flat rectangle or square shape.

What you will need:
* A thin elastic bandage, a blanket or an old pair of tights
* A mix of sizes and weights of balls, including one heavy ball, such as marbles, a cricket ball, a tennis ball
* A partner

2 With the help of your partner, stretch the material quite tight so the fabric can represent your 'space-time'.

3 Roll the smallest, lightest ball across the surface. Adjust your positioning so that the ball follows a straight line. This represents a ray of light travelling through space.

4 Repeat this step but with a heavier ball. You will notice that the heavier ball stretches the material. This represents how space-time becomes curved around heavy objects due to their mass!

5 Now place the heavy ball in the middle of the fabric so it creates a dip in the middle. While the heavy ball is in the middle, roll the smaller balls across the fabric and see what happens.

6 Some of the smaller balls will roll close to the heavy ball – their path becomes bent just like the path of light close to a massive object.

7 Some smaller balls may roll down and fall into the heavy ball. Once it does this, how might it come back out? It can't! This is what would happen with a black hole – their gravity is so strong that light, or anything else, cannot escape.

Train to be an astronaut like
MAE JEMISON

Mae Jemison was born in 1956 in Alabama, USA. As a child, she loved inventing her own science experiments and going to the library to read about space. In 1969, on TV, she watched astronauts landing on the Moon. One day, Jemison told herself, she too would travel to space! None of the astronauts landing on the Moon were Black or female like Jemison, but Lieutenant Uhura on her favourite TV show, *Star Trek*, *did* look like her, so she knew that a different future was possible.

Jemison finished school top of her class and won a scholarship to Stanford University where she studied chemical engineering and African American studies. Some of the other students were mean to Jemison – they didn't think she should study with them because she was Black – but Jemison didn't let that stop her. When she graduated, she became a doctor, travelling around the world to care for people in small villages and refugee camps.

Jemison had not given up on her dream to go to space. When she was 29, she applied to NASA to be an **ASTRONAUT**. Over 2,000 people applied and Jemison was one of just 15 who were accepted. She spent a year in training, taking classes in science, technology and engineering, and learning how to live in microgravity.

NOW IT'S YOUR TURN!

What you will need:
* A puzzle or building blocks set
* A big pair of gloves

1. Time yourself completing a puzzle or creating a tower of building blocks.

2. Take the pieces apart again.

3. Put on the big gloves.

4. Try the puzzle or building blocks again. How quickly can you complete it? This is just like training to be an astronaut wearing space gloves!

Jemison's dream finally came true in 1992 when she flew on the shuttle *Endeavour*, becoming the first Black woman in space! Jemison and her fellow astronauts spent eight days orbiting Earth 127 times. They conducted many experiments, from observing how frogs and hornets behave in space to studying how their own bodies coped in microgravity.

When you are in orbit you experience microgravity. This means you don't feel the pull of gravity, and you float around. To get used to this, astronauts-in-training fly in a special plane that loops up and down, creating moments of microgravity.

When she returned to Earth, Jemison set up a company that invented new technologies for low-income countries, as well as launching a science camp for young people from disadvantaged backgrounds. She has since won lots of awards, written books and even had a role on *Star Trek*, the TV show that inspired her career!

Test a space-landing like
RITU KARIDHAL

Ritu Karidhal is one of India's 'rocket women', working as an **AEROSPACE ENGINEER** for the ISRO (Indian Space Research Organisation). She was born in 1975 in Lucknow, India. When she was young, Karidhal loved looking up at the sky and wondering what was out there, and she was especially interested in the Moon. Sadly, both her parents died while she was at college and she had to look after her brothers and sisters, but Karidhal was determined to continue her studies.

Karidhal studied physics and became a lecturer at the University of Lucknow, before moving to the Indian Institute of Science in Bangalore to get her masters degree in aerospace engineering. Soon after, Karidhal fulfilled her childhood dream of working at the ISRO, helping with missions to the Moon and Mars!

In 2013, Karidhal's team built *Mangalyaan* – a robotic spacecraft sent to orbit Mars. With this successful mission, India became the fourth nation to send a spacecraft to Mars! Karidhal was the navigation expert, which meant she had to make sure *Mangalyaan* could work by itself in space and respond if something went wrong.

Karidhal also worked on the groundbreaking *Chandrayaan 3* mission to the Moon's South Pole, making India the first country to successfully land there!

Karidhal was awarded the ISRO Young Scientist Award in 2007 and has won many other prizes since. She still works tirelessly to inspire women all over the world, showing them that anyone can succeed in the space industry.

NOW IT'S YOUR TURN!

What you will need:

- An egg
- Junk materials, such as cardboard, bubble wrap, scrap paper, plastic bottles, cotton wool
- String
- A carrier bag
- Sticky tape

1. You are going to make a lander to land your egg safely on Mars! Use the junk materials to create your egg-craft. Think about the shape, the size and how safe the egg will be.

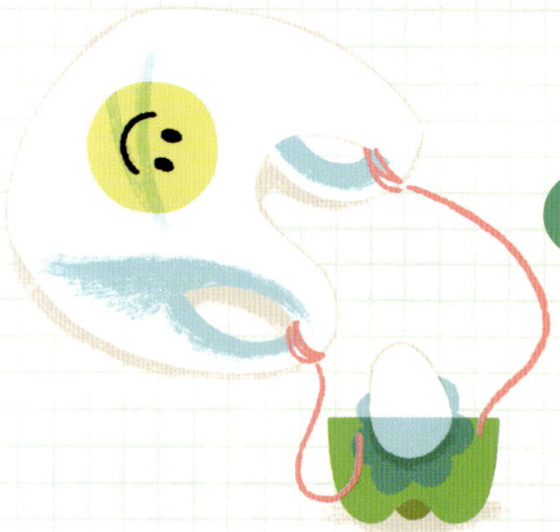

2. Make a parachute from the carrier bag and string, and fix it to the egg lander.

3. Place your egg inside your craft.

4. Now it is test time! Release your egg lander from a window or down an outside stairwell. Make sure to ask a grown-up to help you find a safe place to launch your lander.

5. If your design works, the parachute will slow the fall, and the egg will not smash as it touches the surface of Mars!

6. Did it work? Or do you have to go back to the drawing board and redesign before you test with a new egg?

GLOSSARY

AEROSPACE The Earth's atmosphere and all the space beyond it. Aerospace also refers to the industry that creates things that travel through that space, such as planes and rockets.

ANTIBIOTIC A chemical that slows and stops the growth of bacteria inside the body, taken as a medicine to treat infections.

ANTISEPTIC A chemical that slows and stops the growth of bacteria on the surface of the body, used to clean the skin and reduce the risk of wounds becoming infected.

ASTRONOMY A science that studies everything beyond Earth's atmosphere, including stars, planets and galaxies. Astronomers use physics, maths and chemistry to understand the universe.

ATMOSPHERE A mixture of different gases that surrounds the Earth.

BACTERIA Tiny organisms that are made of just one cell. They are found everywhere on Earth, including on and in our bodies. Some are helpful and some are harmful.

BIODIVERSITY The variety of life in an environment, such as different kinds of animals and plants. An area with a higher number of different species is more biodiverse.

BIOLOGY A science that studies all living things, including animals, plants, fungi, bacteria and all the tiny cells that make up life forms.

BLACK HOLE A place in space where gravity is so strong that not even light can escape. Black holes form from the remains of massive stars that explode when they die.

BOTANY A science that studies plants. Botany is a type of biology. Botanists research how plants grow, how they are structured and how they are used.

CHEMISTRY A science that studies what everything on Earth and in space is made of. Chemists study how substances are structured, how they change and how they interact with each other in chemical reactions.

CLIMATE CHANGE Long term changes in the Earth's weather patterns, such as global warming today. Global warming means that average temperatures across Earth are getting higher.

CONDENSATION The process where a gas turns into a liquid. This mostly happens when the gas is cooled.

CONSERVATION Taking care of our ecosystems. Conservation involves being careful with Earth's resources, such as water and wood, and protecting environments from destruction.

COSMOLOGY A science that studies how the universe began, how it has changed and how it might end. Cosmologists use astronomy and physics in their research.

DENSITY Density is a measure of how tightly packed together the matter (material) is inside an object.

DIAGNOSIS The process of identifying a disease, illness or injury from its signs and symptoms.

DNA The chemical code inside all of us that tells each cell in our bodies how to grow and how to behave, like an instruction manual.

ELECTRICITY The flow of energy that comes from the movement of tiny particles called 'electrons'. A lightning bolt, for example, is a natural spark of electricity.

ENGINEERING A science that studies how we can design and build structures, machines and technologies to solve problems. There are lots of types of engineering, such as aeronautical (focusing on aircraft), aerospace (focusing on spacecraft), chemical and electrical engineering.

ETHOLOGY A science that studies animal behaviour. Ethologists often study animals in their natural habitats.

EVOLUTION The process where living things gradually adapt and change to survive better in their environment. This happens slowly, over many generations.

EVAPORATION The process where liquid turns into a gas. This mostly happens when the liquid is heated.

FORCE The push or pull on an object that makes it move, stop, or change direction and speed.

FOSSIL The remains of an animal or plant that died millions of years ago.

GEOLOGY A science that studies the Earth. Geologists study rocks, fossils, volcanoes and earthquakes, as they try to understand the history and future of our planet.

GRAVITY An invisible force that pulls objects toward bigger objects. On Earth, everything is pulled toward the centre of the planet by the Earth's strong gravity. Gravity is what makes an object fall to the ground when you drop it. It is also what pulls the planets in our solar system into orbit around the Sun.

MASS The amount of matter (material) that makes up an object.

MATHS A science that studies and uses numbers to understand how the world works.

MEDICINE A science that studies health, including preventing, diagnosing and treating illnesses. Doctors who practice medicine are sometimes called 'physicians'.

MICROBIOLOGY A science that studies microorganisms, which are living organisms that are so tiny that you need a microscope to see them.

MOULD A form of fungus. Mould grows on living things, and needs water and oxygen to form.

MUTATION A change in a living thing's DNA. Mutations can be random, or a result of damage to DNA. Some mutations have no effect on the living thing, some are harmful and some are helpful.

ORBIT A repeating path that one object takes around another in space, like the Earth orbiting the Sun.

PALAEONTOLOGY A science that studies the history of life on Earth through fossils.

PHYSICS A science that studies matter (the stuff everything is made of) and energy (which makes things move or change), and the effect they have on each other. Physicists try to understand the laws of nature.

SPACE-TIME A way to think about space and time all together, combining the three dimensions of space (up and down, left and right, forward and backward) with the dimension of time.

SPEED OF LIGHT How fast light travels. It is the fastest possible speed that anything in the universe can travel.

SUPERSONIC Faster than the speed of sound.

VOLCANOLOGY A science that studies volcanoes. Volcanologists study how volcanoes form, how they erupt, how to predict them and the effects they have.

VOLUME How much space an object takes up.

WAVELENGTH The distance between two peaks in a wave, such as a wave of light.

X-RAY Powerful waves of energy that can be used to take pictures of the inside of your body, such as your bones.

ABOUT THE AUTHOR AND ILLUSTRATOR

DR SHEILA KANANI

Dr Sheila Kanani MBE is a planetary scientist, EDI consultant, space educator and author, with a background in astrophysics and astronomy research from UK universities. She regularly acts as a science ambassador, visiting schools and speaking at events, and is an advocate for diversity in physics and astronomy. Sheila runs her company Her Place For Space from home, and enjoys walking on her local beach with her family of boys, playing sports, gazing at the stars, reading and eating (preferably reading whilst eating!).

ELLEN SURREY

Ellen Surrey is an illustrator out of sunny Los Angeles, USA. Endlessly inspired by the surrounding film industry, mid-century design and vintage treasures, Ellen's work presents a vibrant world of joy and whimsy. She has illustrated many books about inspiring people, including one on Audrey Hepburn. Her work has appeared in *The New York Times*, the *Los Angeles Times* and even on a USPS postage stamp. When she isn't working, Ellen enjoys watching old movies and treasure hunting at her favourite vintage markets.

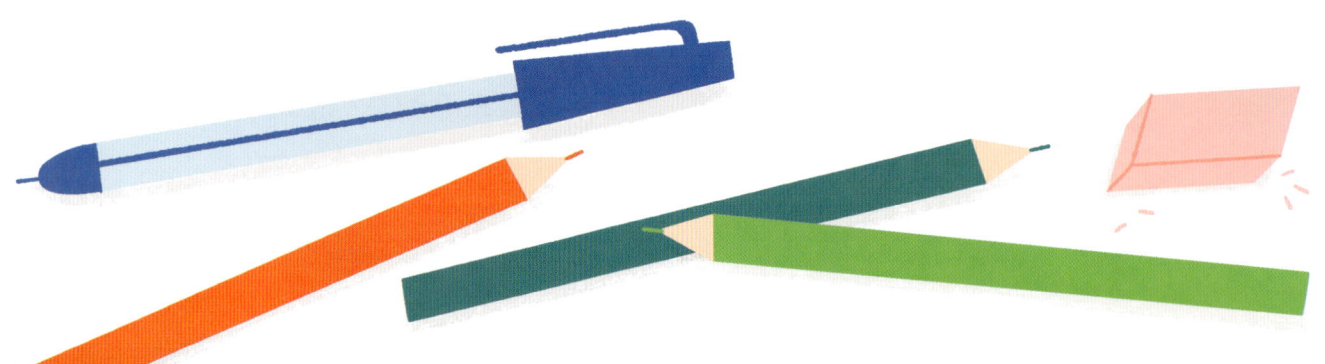